Notebook ATLAS
and Fact Guide

School Specialty
Children's Publishing

Copyright © 2003 School Specialty Children's Publishing. Published by American Education Publishing™, an imprint of School Specialty Children's Publishing, a member of the School Specialty Family.

Send all inquiries to:
School Specialty Children's Publishing
8720 Orion Place
Columbus, OH 43240-2111

ISBN 1-57768-448-6

2 3 4 5 6 7 8 9 10 QPD 09 08 07 06 05 04

ALMANAC

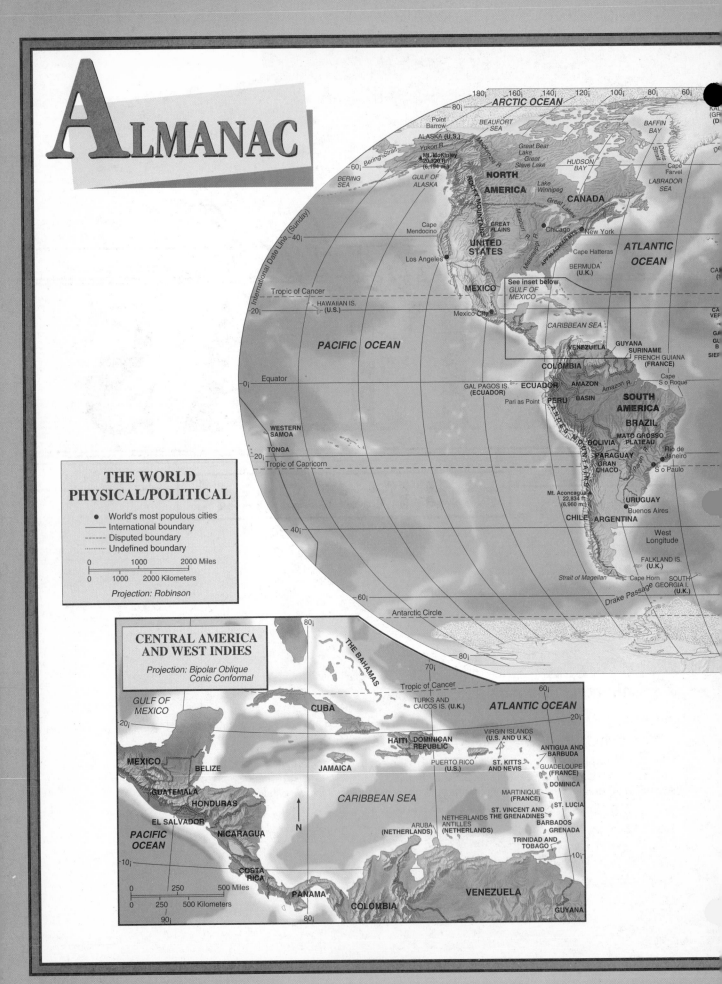

THE WORLD PHYSICAL/POLITICAL

- ● World's most populous cities
- ── International boundary
- ─── Disputed boundary
- ⋯⋯ Undefined boundary

| 0 | 1000 | 2000 Miles |
| 0 | 1000 | 2000 Kilometers |

Projection: Robinson

CENTRAL AMERICA AND WEST INDIES

Projection: Bipolar Oblique Conic Conformal

| 0 | 250 | 500 Miles |
| 0 | 250 | 500 Kilometers |

Map labels (The World):

ARCTIC OCEAN
BEAUFORT SEA
Point Barrow
ALASKA (U.S.)
Yukon R.
Bering Strait
Mt. McKinley 20,320 ft. (6,194 m)
Mackenzie R.
Great Bear Lake
Great Slave Lake
HUDSON BAY
BAFFIN BAY
Davis Strait
Cape Farvel
LABRADOR SEA
BERING SEA
GULF OF ALASKA
ROCKY MOUNTAINS
NORTH AMERICA
Lake Winnipeg
CANADA
Great Lakes
Cape Mendocino
GREAT PLAINS
Missouri R.
Chicago
New York
UNITED STATES
Mississippi R.
APPALACHIAN MTS.
Cape Hatteras
ATLANTIC OCEAN
International Date Line (Sunday)
Los Angeles
BERMUDA (U.K.)
Tropic of Cancer
MEXICO
See inset below
GULF OF MEXICO
HAWAIIAN IS. (U.S.)
Mexico City
CARIBBEAN SEA
PACIFIC OCEAN
GUYANA
VENEZUELA
SURINAME
FRENCH GUIANA (FRANCE)
COLOMBIA
Equator
GALAPAGOS IS. (ECUADOR)
ECUADOR
AMAZON BASIN
Amazon R.
Cape S o Roque
Parías Point
PERU
SOUTH AMERICA
BRAZIL
WESTERN SAMOA
ANDES MOUNTAINS
MATO GROSSO PLATEAU
TONGA
BOLIVIA
Rio de Janeiro
Tropic of Capricorn
PARAGUAY
GRAN CHACO
S o Paulo
Mt. Aconcagua 22,834 ft. (6,960 m)
URUGUAY
Buenos Aires
CHILE
ARGENTINA
West Longitude
FALKLAND IS. (U.K.)
Strait of Magellan
Cape Horn
SOUTH GEORGIA I. (U.K.)
Drake Passage
Antarctic Circle

Map labels (Central America and West Indies):

THE BAHAMAS
Tropic of Cancer
TURKS AND CAICOS IS. (U.K.)
ATLANTIC OCEAN
GULF OF MEXICO
CUBA
MEXICO
BELIZE
HAITI
DOMINICAN REPUBLIC
VIRGIN ISLANDS (U.S. AND U.K.)
ANTIGUA AND BARBUDA
JAMAICA
PUERTO RICO (U.S.)
ST. KITTS AND NEVIS
GUADELOUPE (FRANCE)
DOMINICA
GUATEMALA
CARIBBEAN SEA
MARTINIQUE (FRANCE)
ST. LUCIA
HONDURAS
ST. VINCENT AND THE GRENADINES
EL SALVADOR
NETHERLANDS ANTILLES (NETHERLANDS)
ARUBA (NETHERLANDS)
BARBADOS
GRENADA
PACIFIC OCEAN
NICARAGUA
TRINIDAD AND TOBAGO
COSTA RICA
PANAMA
VENEZUELA
COLOMBIA
GUYANA
N

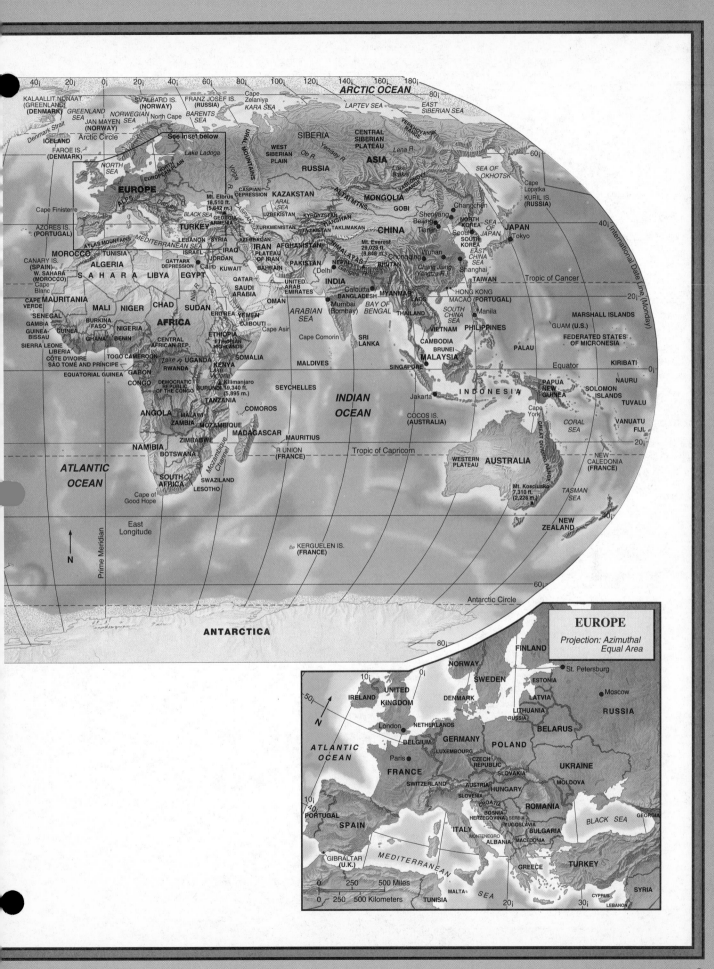

ARCTIC OCEAN

40j 20j 0j 20j 40j 60j 80j 100j 120j 140j 160j 180j

KALAALLIT NUNAAT
(GREENLAND)
(DENMARK)
GREENLAND
SEA
JAN MAYEN
(NORWAY)
SVALBARD IS.
(NORWAY)
FRANZ JOSEF IS.
(RUSSIA)
Cape
Zelaniya
KARA SEA
LAPTEV SEA
EAST
SIBERIAN SEA
80j

ICELAND
NORWEGIAN
SEA
North Cape
BARENTS
SEA
SIBERIA
CENTRAL
SIBERIAN
PLATEAU
VERKHOYANSK
RANGE

Denmark Strait
Arctic Circle
See Inset below
WEST
SIBERIAN
PLAIN
Ob R.
Yenisey R.
Lena R.
Lake
Baikal
60j

FAROE IS.
(DENMARK)
NORTH
SEA
Lake Ladoga
URAL MOUNTAINS
RUSSIA
ASIA
SEA OF
OKHOTSK
Cape
Lopatka

Cape Finisterre
EUROPE
EUROPEAN PLAIN
Volga
CASPIAN
DEPRESSION
KAZAKHSTAN
MONGOLIA
YASLONOVY RANGE
KURIL IS.
(RUSSIA)
40j

AZORES IS.
(PORTUGAL)
ALPS
Danube R.
Mt. Elbrus
18,510 ft.
(5,642 m.)
ARAL
SEA
GOBI
Changchun
Shenyang
NORTH
KOREA
SEA
OF
JAPAN
JAPAN

MOROCCO
TURKEY
BLACK SEA
GEORGIA
ARMENIA
UZBEKISTAN
KYRGYZSTAN
TANSHAN
Beijing
Tianjin
Seoul
SOUTH
KOREA
EAST
CHINA
SEA
Tokyo

ATLAS MOUNTAINS
MEDITERRANEAN SEA
LEBANON SYRIA
AZERBAIJAN
TURKMENISTAN
TAJIKISTAN
TAKLIMAKAN
CHINA
Mt. Everest
29,028 ft.
(8,848 m.)
Chongqing
Wuhan
Chang Jiang
(Yangtze R.)
Shanghai

CANARY IS.
(SPAIN)
TUNISIA
ISRAEL
IRAQ
JORDAN
IRAN
PLATEAU
OF IRAN
AFGHANISTAN
HIMALAYAS
NEPAL
Ganges R.
BHUTAN
TAIWAN
Tropic of Cancer
20j

W. SAHARA
(MOROCCO)
ALGERIA
LIBYA
EGYPT
QATTARA
DEPRESSION
Cairo
Nile R.
KUWAIT
BAHRAIN
QATAR
UNITED
ARAB
EMIRATES
PAKISTAN
Delhi
INDIA
Calcutta
BANGLADESH
MYANMAR
LAOS
HONG KONG
MACAO (PORTUGAL)

Cape
Blanc
S A H A R A
SAUDI
ARABIA
OMAN
ARABIAN
SEA
Mumbai
(Bombay)
BAY OF
BENGAL
THAILAND
VIETNAM
SOUTH
CHINA
SEA
Manila
MARSHALL ISLANDS

CAPE
VERDE
MAURITANIA
MALI
NIGER
CHAD
SUDAN
ERITREA
YEMEN
DJIBOUTI
Cape Asir
Cape Comorin
SRI
LANKA
CAMBODIA
PHILIPPINES
GUAM (U.S.)
FEDERATED STATES
OF MICRONESIA

SENEGAL
GAMBIA
GUINEA-
BISSAU
BURKINA
FASO
NIGERIA
BENIN
AFRICA
CENTRAL
AFRICAN REP.
ETHIOPIA
ETHIOPIAN
HIGHLANDS
SOMALIA
MALDIVES
BRUNEI
MALAYSIA
PALAU

SIERRA LEONE
GUINEA
GHANA
TOGO
CAMEROON
UGANDA
KENYA
SINGAPORE
Equator
KIRIBATI
0j

LIBERIA
CÔTE D'IVOIRE
SÃO TOMÉ AND PRÍNCIPE
GABON
Zaire R.
RWANDA
Lake
Victoria
SEYCHELLES
INDIAN
OCEAN
Jakarta
I N D O N E S I A
PAPUA
NEW
GUINEA
NAURU
SOLOMON
ISLANDS

EQUATORIAL GUINEA
CONGO
DEMOCRATIC
REPUBLIC
OF THE CONGO
BURUNDI
Kilimanjaro
19,340 ft.
(5,895 m.)
TANZANIA
Cape
York
CORAL
SEA
TUVALU

ANGOLA
MALAWI
ZAMBIA
COMOROS
MADAGASCAR
MAURITIUS
COCOS IS.
(AUSTRALIA)
VANUATU
FIJI

NAMIBIA
ZIMBABWE
MOZAMBIQUE
Mozambique
Channel
R UNION
(FRANCE)
Tropic of Capricorn
20j

ATLANTIC
OCEAN
BOTSWANA
WESTERN
PLATEAU
AUSTRALIA
GREAT DIVIDING RANGE
NEW
CALEDONIA
(FRANCE)

SOUTH
AFRICA
SWAZILAND
LESOTHO
Mt. Kosciusko
7,310 ft.
(2,228 m.)
TASMAN
SEA

Cape of
Good Hope
East
Longitude
KERGUELEN IS.
(FRANCE)
NEW
ZEALAND
40j

N
Prime Meridian
60j

Antarctic Circle

80j

ANTARCTICA

See Inset below

EUROPE
Projection: Azimuthal
Equal Area

FINLAND
St. Petersburg
NORWAY
SWEDEN
ESTONIA
Moscow
IRELAND
UNITED
KINGDOM
DENMARK
LATVIA
LITHUANIA
RUSSIA
RUSSIA
50j
London
NETHERLANDS
GERMANY
BELARUS
BELGIUM
POLAND
ATLANTIC
OCEAN
Paris
LUXEMBOURG
CZECH
REPUBLIC
UKRAINE
FRANCE
SLOVAKIA
MOLDOVA
SWITZERLAND
AUSTRIA
HUNGARY
10j
40j
SLOVENIA
ROMANIA
PORTUGAL
CROATIA
BOSNIA
HERZEGOVINA
SERBIA
YUGOSLAVIA
BLACK
SEA
GEORGIA
SPAIN
ITALY
MONTENEGRO
BULGARIA
ALBANIA
MACEDONIA
N
GIBRALTAR
(U.K.)
MEDITERRANEAN
GREECE
TURKEY
0 250 500 Miles
MALTA
SEA
CYPRUS
SYRIA
0 250 500 Kilometers
TUNISIA
20j
30j
LEBANON

3

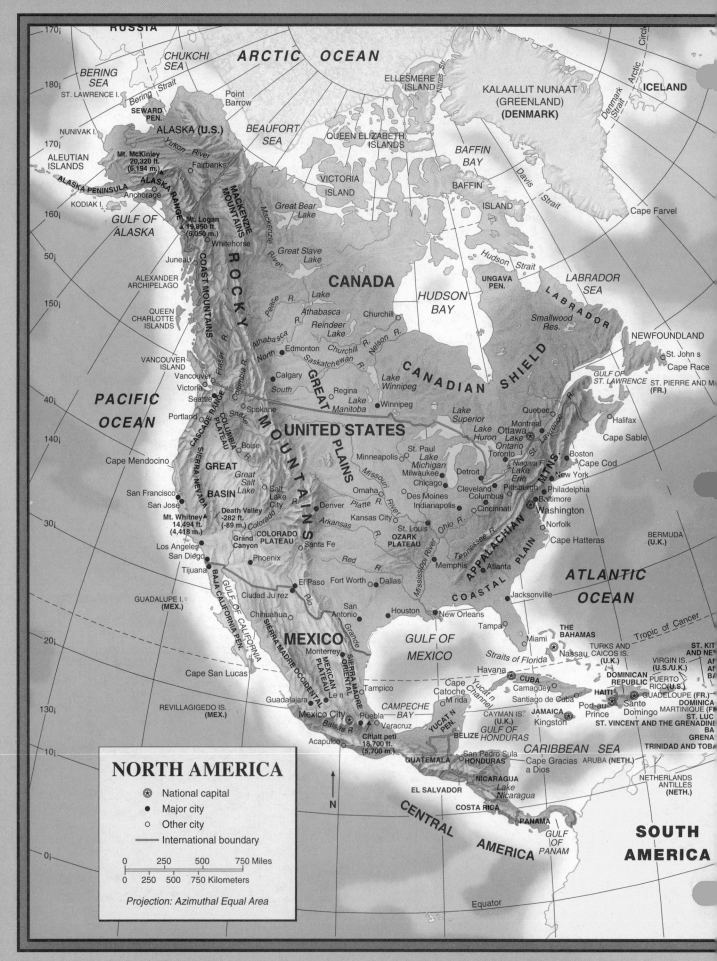

NORTH AMERICA

⊛ National capital
● Major city
○ Other city
── International boundary

0   250   500   750 Miles
0 250 500 750 Kilometers

Projection: Azimuthal Equal Area

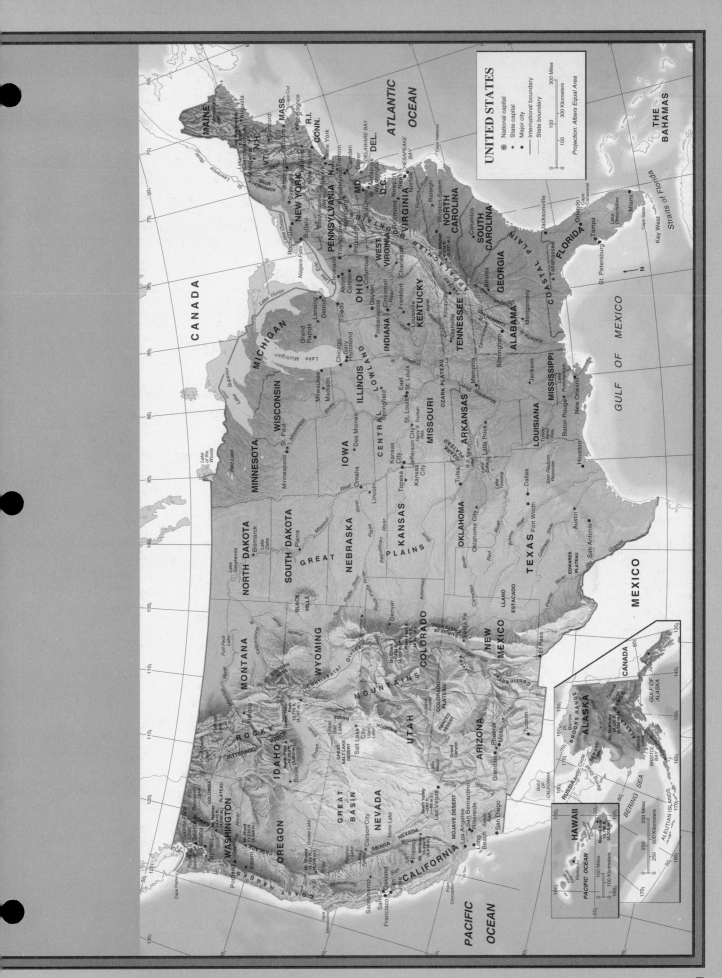

North America

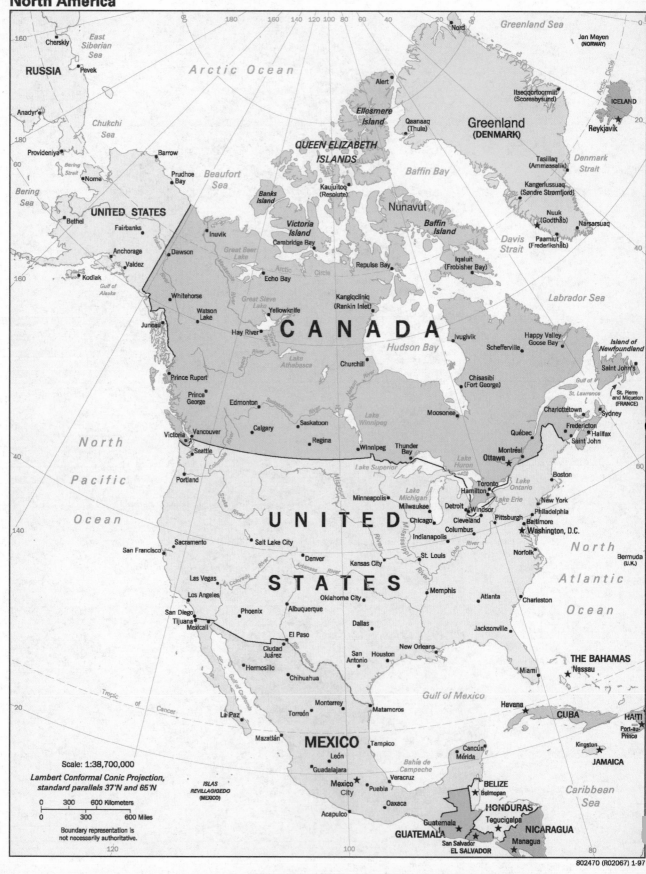

Scale: 1:38,700,000

Lambert Conformal Conic Projection,
standard parallels 37°N and 65°N

| 0 | 300 | 600 Kilometers |
| 0 | 300 | 600 Miles |

Boundary representation is
not necessarily authoritative.

802470 (R02067) 1-97

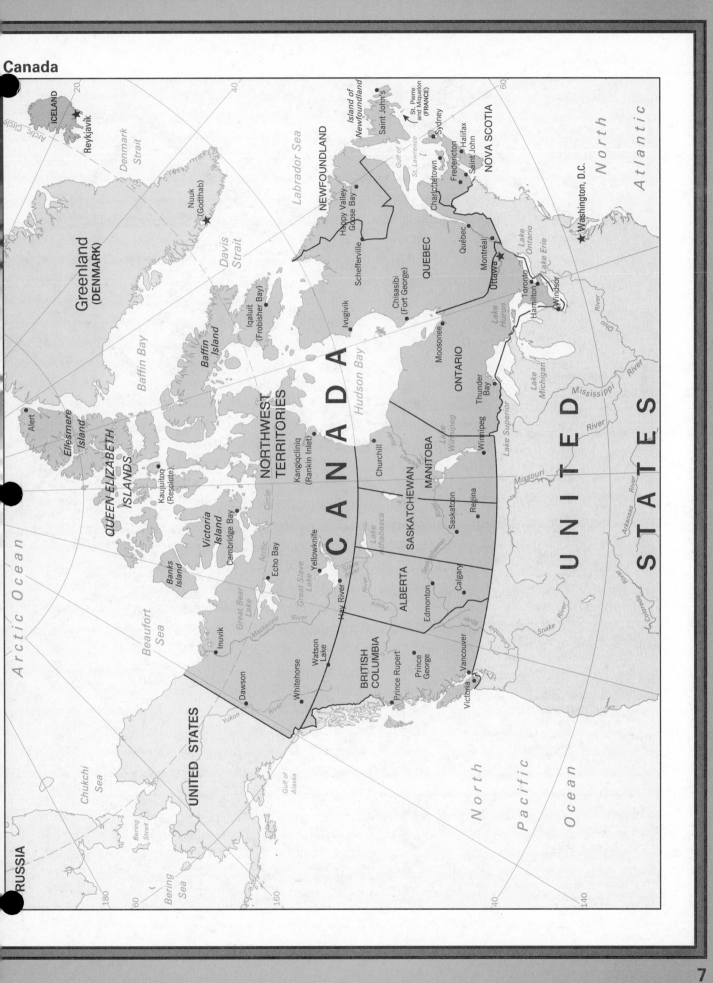

UNITED STATES

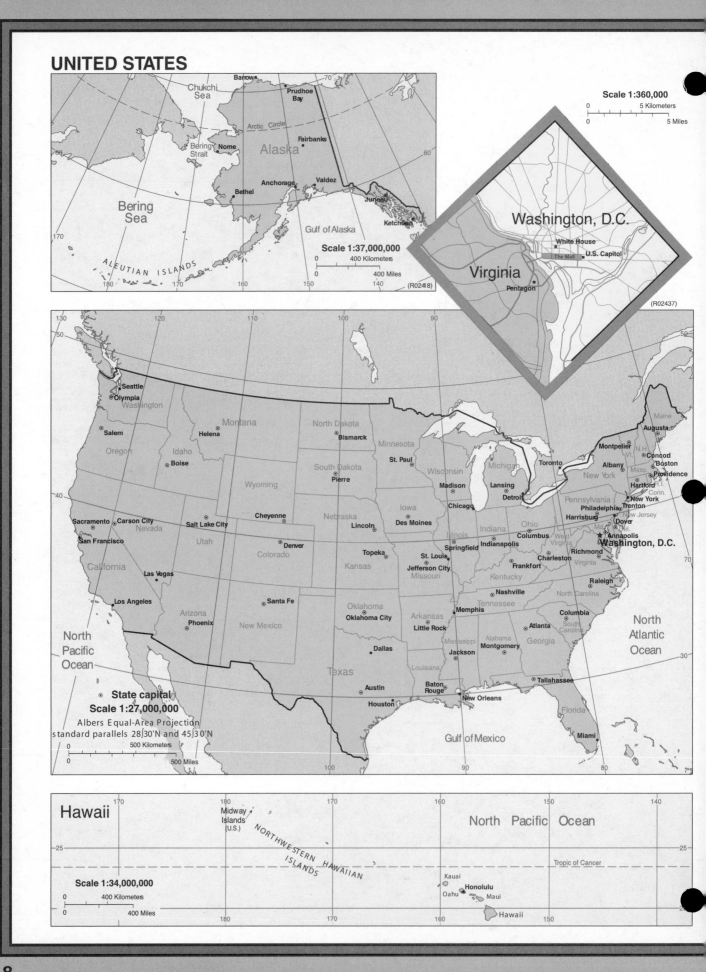

Scale 1:360,000

0   5 Kilometers
0   5 Miles

Chukchi Sea
Barrow
Prudhoe Bay
70
Arctic Circle
Alaska
Fairbanks
60
Bering Strait
Nome
Anchorage
Valdez
Bethel
Juneau
Bering Sea
Ketchikan
Gulf of Alaska
ALEUTIAN ISLANDS
Scale 1:37,000,000
0   400 Kilometers
0   400 Miles
170   180   170   160   150   140
(R02418)

Washington, D.C.
White House
The Mall
U.S. Capitol
Virginia
Pentagon
(R02437)

130   120   110   100   90   50
50
Seattle
Olympia
Washington
Salem
Montana
North Dakota
Bismarck
Minnesota
Augusta
Maine
Oregon
Helena
Idaho
St. Paul
Wisconsin
Michigan
Toronto
Montpelier
Concord
N.H.
Boise
South Dakota
Pierre
Madison
Lansing
Albany
Boston
Mass.
Providence
40
Wyoming
Iowa
Chicago
Detroit
New York
Hartford
Conn.
Sacramento
Carson City
Nevada
Salt Lake City
Cheyenne
Nebraska
Lincoln
Des Moines
Illinois
Indiana
Ohio
Columbus
Pennsylvania
Harrisburg
New York
Philadelphia
Trenton
New Jersey
Dover
Del.
Annapolis
Md.
San Francisco
Utah
Denver
Colorado
Topeka
Springfield
Indianapolis
Richmond
Washington, D.C.
California
Las Vegas
Kansas
St. Louis
Jefferson City
Missouri
Frankfort
Charleston
West Virginia
Virginia
70
Kentucky
Raleigh
Los Angeles
Santa Fe
Nashville
North Carolina
Arizona
New Mexico
Oklahoma
Oklahoma City
Memphis
Tennessee
Columbia
South Carolina
Phoenix
Little Rock
Arkansas
Atlanta
Alabama
Georgia
North Atlantic Ocean
North Pacific Ocean
Dallas
Mississippi
Montgomery
30
Texas
Jackson
Louisiana
● **State capital**
Scale 1:27,000,000
Albers Equal-Area Projection
standard parallels 28°30'N and 45°30'N
Austin
Baton Rouge
Tallahassee
Houston
New Orleans
Florida
0   500 Kilometers
0   500 Miles
Gulf of Mexico
Miami
100   90   80

Hawaii
170   180   170   160   150   140
Midway Islands (U.S.)
North Pacific Ocean
NORTHWESTERN HAWAIIAN ISLANDS
25
25
Tropic of Cancer
Scale 1:34,000,000
Kauai
Honolulu
0   400 Kilometers
Oahu
Maui
0   400 Miles
Hawaii
180   170   160   150

8

South America

Caribbean Sea

Isla de
San Andrés
(COLOMBIA)

Martinique (FRANCE)
ST. LUCIA
ST. VINCENT AND
THE GRENADINES
GRENADA
BARBADOS

North
Atlantic
Ocean

Barranquilla
Cartagena
Maracaibo
Aruba
(NETH.)
Netherlands
Antilles
(NETH.)
Caracas
Valencia
Port-of-Spain
TRINIDAD AND
TOBAGO

Barquisimeto

Cúcuta
San Cristóbal
Medellín
VENEZUELA
Ciudad
Guayana
Georgetown
Paramaribo
Cayenne
GUYANA
SURINAME
French
Guiana
(FRANCE)

Isla de Malpelo
(COLOMBIA)
Bogotá
Cali
COLOMBIA
Rio Magdalena
Río Orinoco
Boa Vista
Macapá

Equator
Quito
ECUADOR
Guayaquil
Iquitos
Amazon
Rio Negro
Amazon
Manaus
Santarém
Belém
São Luís
Fortaleza

Piura
Trujillo
Rio Marañón
Huánuco
Río Branco
Pôrto
Velho
Rio Madeira
BRAZIL
Teresina
Natal
Recife

PERU
Lima
Rio Ucayali
Rio Beni
Cusco
Lago
Titicaca
Rio Mamoré
Trinidad
Cuiabá
Brasília
Goiânia
Rio Tocantins
Rio Xingu
São Francisco
Maceió
Salvador

Arequipa
La Paz
BOLIVIA
Cochabamba
Sucre
Santa Cruz
Arica
Potosí
Rio Paraguai
Uberlândia
Belo
Horizonte

South
Pacific
Ocean

Iquique
Campo
Grande
Vitória

Tropic of Capricorn
Antofagasta
PARAGUAY
Asunción
Rio Paraná
Rio de Janeiro
São Paulo
Santos

Isla San Félix
(CHILE)
Isla San Ambrosio
(CHILE)
Salta
San Miguel
de Tucumán
Resistencia
Rio Paraná
Curitiba
Florianópolis

ARCHIPIÉLAGO
JUAN FERNANDEZ
(CHILE)
CHILE
Córdoba
Santa Fe
Salto
Pôrto Alegre

Valparaíso
Mendoza
Rosario
URUGUAY
Santiago
Buenos Aires
La Plata
Montevideo

South
Atlantic
Ocean

Concepción
ARGENTINA
Bahía Blanca
Mar del Plata

Puerto Montt
San Carlos de
Bariloche

Comodoro Rivadavia

Scale 1:35,000,000
Azimuthal Equal-Area Projection

0   500 Kilometers
0   500 Miles

Boundary representation is
not necessarily authoritative.

Río
Gallegos
Strait of
Magellan
Stanley
Falkland Islands
(Islas Malvinas)

Punta Arenas
Ushuaia

South Georgia and the
South Sandwich Islands

Europe

Serbia and Montenegro have asserted the formation
of a joint independent state, but this entity has
not been formally recognized as a state by the
United States.

F.Y.R.O.M. - The Former Yugoslav Republic of Macedonia

Greenland
(DENMARK)

Jan Mayen
(NORWAY)

Greenland
Sea

*Denmark
Strait*

Norwegian Sea

Hammerfest

Tromsø

Murmansk

*Barents
Sea*

Arctic   Circle

Kiruna

White Sea

Arkhangel'sk

Reykjavík ★ ICELAND

NORWAY

Luleå

Oulu

Severnaya
Dvina

Tórshavn Faroe Islands
(DENMARK)

Trondheim

SWEDEN

Umeå

FINLAND

Lake
Onega

Lake
Ladoga

Rockall
(U.K.)

SHETLAND
ISLANDS

Bergen

*Gulf
of
Bothnia*

Gävle

Tampere

Helsinki

Turku

ÅLAND
ISLANDS

Gulf of Finland

St. Petersburg

RUSSIA

Oslo ★

Stockholm ★

Tallinn ★

ESTONIA

Volga

Moscow

*North
Atlantic*

HEBRIDES

ORKNEY
ISLANDS

Stavanger

Göteborg

Gotland

Skagerrak

LATVIA

Rīga ★

Vitsyebsk

Smolensk

Ocean

Aberdeen

Glasgow

Edinburgh

Baltic Sea

Öland

LITHUANIA

Vilnius ★

Mahilyow

Dnyapro

*North
Sea*

DENMARK

Malmö

Kaliningrad

RUSSIA

Minsk ★

UNITED

Belfast

*Irish
Sea*

Isle
of
Man
(U.K.)

Leeds

Manchester

Liverpool

Copenhagen

Bornholm

Gdańsk

Hrodna

BELARUS

Homyel'

Dublin

IRELAND

Hamburg

Bremen

Berlin ★

Poznań

Oder

Warsaw ★

Brest

KINGDOM

Cardiff

Birmingham

Amsterdam

NETH.

Essen

Leipzig

POLAND

Łódź

Wrocław

Kiev

Rivne

L'viv

*Celtic
Sea*

London ★

Rotterdam

Brussels ★

Lille

BEL.

Cologne

Bonn

GERMANY

Frankfurt
am Main

Prague ★

CZECH REPUBLIC

Brno

Kraków

Chernivtsi

UKRAINE

Mykolayiv

English   Channel

Guernsey (U.K.)

Jersey (U.K.)

Paris ★

LUX.

Luxembourg

Stuttgart

Munich

Danube

SLOVAKIA

Bratislava ★

Chişinău

Odesa

Seine

Strasbourg

Rhine

LIECH.

Vaduz ★

Iaşi

MOLDOVA

Nantes

Loire

Zürich

Bern ★

SWITZ.

Geneva

AUSTRIA

Vienna ★

Budapest ★

Cluj-
Napoca

ROMANIA

FRANCE

Lyon

Ljubljana ★

SLOVENIA

Milan

Turin

Venice

Zagreb ★

HUNGARY

Bucharest ★

Constanța

*Bay of
Biscay*

Po

Genoa

CROATIA

BOSNIA AND
HERZEGOVINA

Belgrade ★

Serbia

Danube

*Black
Sea*

Varna

Bordeaux

SAN
MARINO

Florence

Sarajevo ★

Montenegro

BULGARIA

Bilbao

Toulouse

MONACO

*Ligurian
Sea*

Podgorica ★

Sofia ★

Porto

Andorra
la Vella

Marseille

ITALY

Rome ★

*Adriatic
Sea*

Skopje ★

F.Y.R.O.M.

Thessaloníki

Zaragoza

ANDORRA

Corsica
(FRANCE)

VATICAN
CITY

Tirane ★

ALB.

PORTUGAL

Madrid ★

Barcelona

*Balearic
Sea*

Sardinia

Naples

*Aegean
Sea*

GREECE

Lisbon ★

SPAIN

Valencia

BALEARIC
ISLANDS

*Tyrrhenian
Sea*

Athens ★

Tagus

Sevilla

Cagliari

*Ionian
Sea*

Rhodes

Gibraltar
(U.K.)

Málaga

Palermo

Sicily

Crete

Strait of Gibraltar

*Alborán
Sea*

Mediterranean Sea

Scale 1: 19,500,000

Lambert Conformal Conic Projection,
standard parallels 40 N and 56 N

MALTA ★ Valletta

0   300 Kilometers
0   20   300 Miles

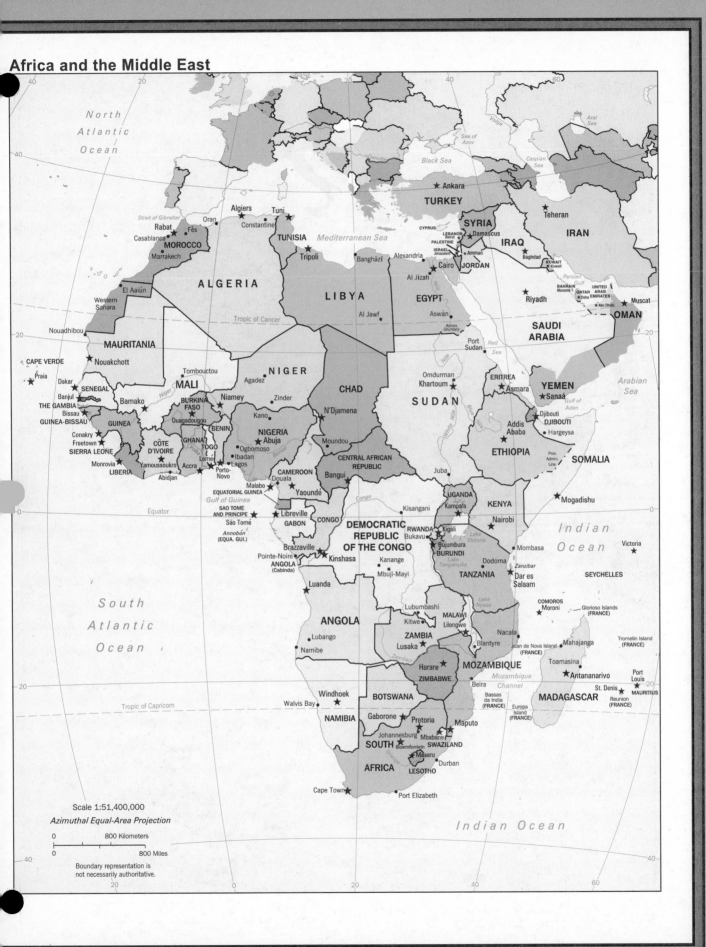

Scale 1:51,400,000

Azimuthal Equal-Area Projection

0 — 800 Kilometers
0 — 800 Miles

Boundary representation is
not necessarily authoritative.

Norwegian Sea
North Sea
Barents Sea
Arctic Ocean
East Siberian Sea
Bering Sea
Kara Sea
Laptev Sea
Arctic Circle
Lake Ladoga
Lake Onega
Sea of Okhotsk
Pechora
Ob
Volga
Kama
Irtysh
Yenisey
Lena
Angara
Vilyuy
Amur
Kolyma

Black Sea
GEORGIA
T'bilisi
ARMENIA
Yerevan
AZERBAIJAN
Baku
Caspian Sea
Atyrau
Aqmola
Qaraghandy
KAZAKSTAN
Aral Sea
Lake Balkhash
Lake Baikal
Tabrīz
Tehrān
TURKMENISTAN
UZBEKISTAN
Ashgabat
Tashkent
Bishkek
KYRGYZSTAN
Almaty
Ulaanbaatar
MONGOLIA
Harbin
Changchun
Shenyang
Sapporo
Sea of Japan
JAPAN
Tokyo
NORTH KOREA
Pyŏngyang
Yokohama
Nagoya
Osaka
Esfahān
Mashhad
Dushanbe
TAJIKISTAN
Kashi
Ürümqi
Baotou
Beijing
Dalian
Demarcation Line
Seoul
SOUTH KOREA
Pusan
Fukuoka
IRAN
Shīrāz
Kābul
AFGHANISTAN
Line of Control
Chinese line of control
Tianjin
Jinan
Taiyuan
Qingdao
Yellow Sea
Bandar-e 'Abbās
Qandahār
Islāmābād
Quetta
Lahore
Indian claim
Lanzhou
Xi'an
Zhengzhou
Nanjing
Shanghai
East China Sea
CHINA
Persian Gulf
PAKISTAN
New Delhi
NEPAL
Lhasa
BHUTAN
Thimphu
Chengdu
Changsha
Wuhan
Hangzhou
Nanchang
RYUKYU ISLANDS
Okinawa
Karāchi
Jaipur
Lucknow
Kānpur
Kathmandu
Chongqing
Guiyang
Taipei
Tropic of Cancer
Taiwan
Ahmadābād
BANGLADESH
Dhaka
Ganges
Brahmaputra
Kunming
Xi Jiang
Guangzhou
Chang Jiang
Surat
Calcutta
Chittagong
Mandalay
Hanoi
Nanning
Hong Kong (U.K.)
Macau (PORT.)
Philippine Sea
Mumbai (Bombay)
Pune
Nāgpur
INDIA
BURMA
LAOS
Haiphong
Hainan Dao
Hyderābād
Vientiane
Hue
South China Sea
Luzon
Manila
Arabian Sea
Rangoon
THAILAND
VIETNAM
PHILIPPINES
Bangalore
Chennai (Madras)
Bay of Bengal
Bangkok
Cebu
LAKSHADWEEP (INDIA)
ANDAMAN ISLANDS (INDIA)
Andaman Sea
CAMBODIA
SPRATLY ISLANDS
Mindano
Davao
Jaffna
Phnom Penh
Ho Chi Minh City
Sulu Sea
Laccadive Sea
SRI LANKA
NICOBAR ISLANDS (INDIA)
Gulf of Thailand
Bandar Seri Begawan
BRUNEI
Celebes Sea
MALDIVES
Colombo
Male
MALAYSIA
Kuala Lumpur
MALAYSIA
Borneo
Medan
Singapore
SINGAPORE
Pontianak
Celebes
Banda Sea
Equator
Sumatra
Ujungpandang
INDONESIA
Palembang
Jakarta
Java Sea
Surabaya
Timor
Bandung
Semarang
Java
Timor Sea
Indian Ocean

Scale 1:48,000,000
Azimuthal Equal-Area Projection

0   800 Kilometers
0   800 Miles

Boundary representation is
not necessarily authoritative.

20 40 60 80 100 120 140 160 180

North Pacific Ocean

South Pacific Ocean

CHINA
Guangzhou
Shantou
Xiamen
Fuzhou
Wenzhou
Taipei
TAIWAN
Kao-hsiung
Hong Kong (U.K.)
Macau (PORT.)

PHILIPPINES
Luzon
Manila
Samar
Panay
Cebu
Bacolod
Iloilo
Negros
Zamboanga
Cagayan de Oro
Davao
Mindanao

RYUKYU ISLANDS (JAPAN)
Okinawa
Okino-tori-shima (JAPAN)
DAITŌ-SHOTŌ (JAPAN)

NAMPO-SHOTŌ
BONIN ISLANDS (JAPAN)
VOLCANO ISLANDS (JAPAN)

Marcus Island (JAPAN)

Philippine Sea

South China Sea

INDONESIA
Palawan
Bandar Seri Begawan
BRUNEI
MALAYSIA
Borneo
Samarinda
Banjarmasin
Sulawesi
Manado
Halmahera
Ceram
Buru
Ambon
Sorong
Jayapura
New Guinea

Celebes Sea
Sulu Sea
Molucca Sea
Banda Sea
Timor Sea
Arafura Sea
Java Sea

Ujungpandang
Surabaya
Bali
Denpasar
Lombok
Sumbawa
Flores
Timor
Sumba
Kupang
Ashmore and Cartier Islands (AUSTRALIA)

PALAU
Koror
Yap

FEDERATED STATES OF MICRONESIA
CAROLINE ISLANDS
Pohnpei
Kolonia

Northern Mariana Islands (U.S.)
Saipan
Guam (U.S.)
Agana

MARSHALL ISLANDS
Majuro
Kwajalein
Enewetak
Wake Island (U.S.)

Equator

Tropic of Cancer

HAWAIIAN ISLANDS
Midway Islands (U.S.)
Kauai
Oahu
Honolulu
Maui
Hawaii
UNITED STATES
Hawaii

Johnston Atoll (U.S.)
Kingman Reef (U.S.)
Palmyra Atoll (U.S.)
Howland Island (U.S.)
Baker Island (U.S.)
Jarvis Island (U.S.)

KIRIBATI
Kiritimati (Christmas Island) (KIRIBATI)
LINE ISLANDS

KIRIBATI
KIRIBATI (GILBERT ISLANDS)
Tarawa
Banaba

NAURU
Yaren District

SOLOMON ISLANDS
Bougainville
New Ireland
New Britain
Honiara
Guadalcanal

PAPUA NEW GUINEA
Wewak
Madang
Lae
Port Moresby

TUVALU
Funafuti

RAWAKI (PHOENIX ISLANDS)

Tokelau (N.Z.)
WESTERN SAMOA
Apia
American Samoa (U.S.)
Pago Pago
Wallis and Futuna (FRANCE)
Mata-utu

SANTA CRUZ ISLANDS
VANUATU
Port-Vila

FIJI
Rotuma
Vanua Levu
Viti Levu
Suva

New Caledonia (FRANCE)
Nouméa

TONGA
Nuku'alofa
Niue (N.Z.)
Alofi

Cook Islands (N.Z.)
Avarua

French Polynesia (FRANCE)
SOCIETY ISLANDS
Tahiti
Papeete

ÎLES MARQUISES

ARCHIPEL DES TUAMOTU

ÎLES TUBUAI

Rapa

Pitcairn Islands (U.K.)

Tropic of Capricorn

Minerva Reef

KERMADEC ISLANDS (N.Z.)

CHATHAM ISLANDS (N.Z.)

AUSTRALIA
Darwin
Port Hedland
Mount Isa
Alice Springs
Cairns
Townsville
Mackay
Rockhampton
Gladstone
Brisbane
Gold Coast
Newcastle
Sydney
Wollongong
Canberra
Melbourne
Geelong
Bendigo
Broken Hill
Adelaide
Whyalla
Port Augusta
Kalgoorlie
Perth
Bunbury
Esperance
Geraldton

Gulf of Carpentaria
Great Australian Bight
Great Dividing Range
Murray
Darling

Coral Sea
Coral Sea Islands (AUSTRALIA)

Tasman Sea

Bass Strait
Tasmania
Hobart

Norfolk Island (AUSTRALIA)
Kingston
Lord Howe Island (AUSTRALIA)

NEW ZEALAND
North Island
Auckland
Hamilton
Hastings
Wellington
South Island
Christchurch
Dunedin
Invercargill
Stewart Island

Indian Ocean

Scale: 1:36,000,000 at 30°S
Mercator Projection

0   500 Kilometers
0   500 Miles

World Population Density

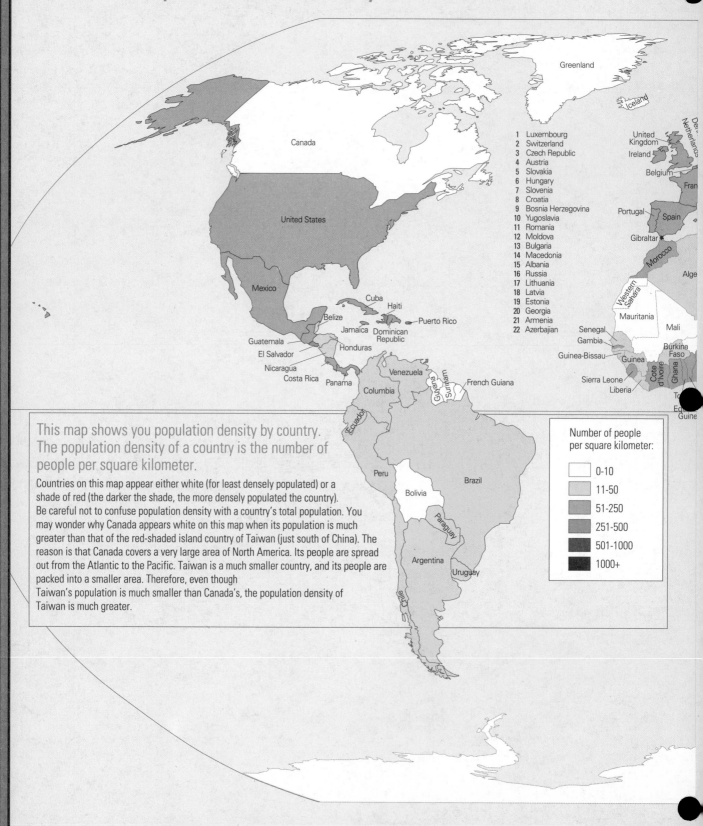

1 Luxembourg
2 Switzerland
3 Czech Republic
4 Austria
5 Slovakia
6 Hungary
7 Slovenia
8 Croatia
9 Bosnia Herzegovina
10 Yugoslavia
11 Romania
12 Moldova
13 Bulgaria
14 Macedonia
15 Albania
16 Russia
17 Lithuania
18 Latvia
19 Estonia
20 Georgia
21 Armenia
22 Azerbaijan

This map shows you population density by country. The population density of a country is the number of people per square kilometer.

Countries on this map appear either white (for least densely populated) or a shade of red (the darker the shade, the more densely populated the country). Be careful not to confuse population density with a country's total population. You may wonder why Canada appears white on this map when its population is much greater than that of the red-shaded island country of Taiwan (just south of China). The reason is that Canada covers a very large area of North America. Its people are spread out from the Atlantic to the Pacific. Taiwan is a much smaller country, and its people are packed into a smaller area. Therefore, even though Taiwan's population is much smaller than Canada's, the population density of Taiwan is much greater.

Number of people per square kilometer:

	0-10
	11-50
	51-250
	251-500
	501-1000
	1000+

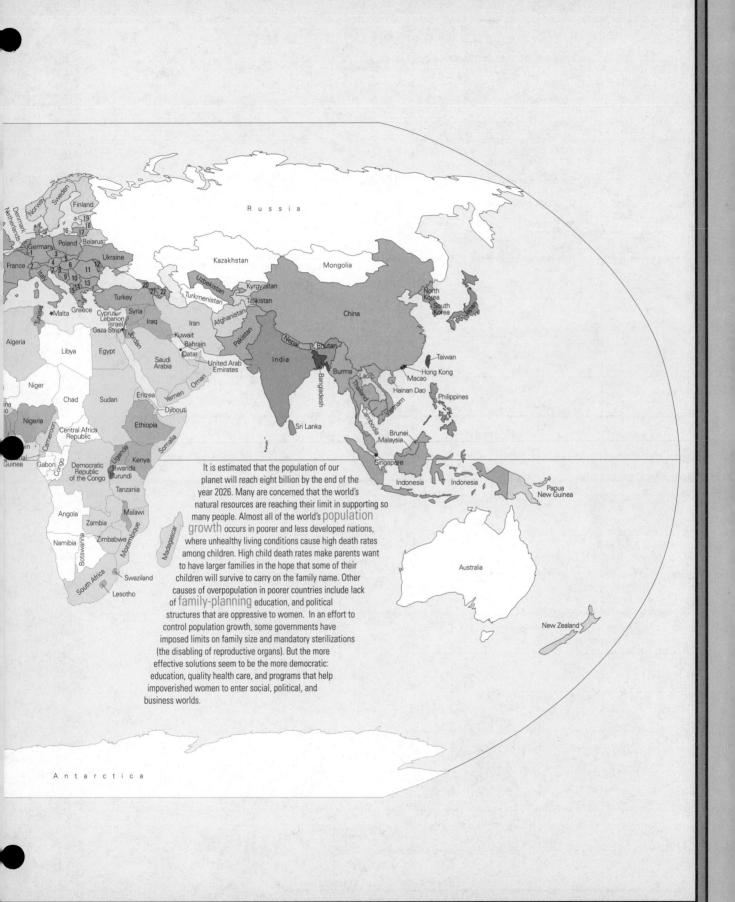

R u s s i a

Norway
Sweden
Finland
Denmark
Netherlands
19
18
16 17
Germany
Poland
Belarus
France
Italy
4
5
Ukraine
3
6
9 11
7 8 12
10 13
14
15
20 21 22
Turkey
Tunisia
Malta
Greece
Cyprus
Lebanon
Syria
Israel
Gaza Strip
Iraq
Jordan
Algeria
Libya
Egypt
Saudi Arabia
Kuwait
Bahrain
Qatar
United Arab Emirates
Oman
Niger
Chad
Sudan
Eritrea
Yemen
Djibouti
Nigeria
Cameroon
Central Africa Republic
Ethiopia
Somalia
Gabon
Congo
Democratic Republic of the Congo
Uganda
Rwanda
Burundi
Kenya
Tanzania
Angola
Zambia
Malawi
Mozambique
Madagascar
Namibia
Botswana
Zimbabwe
South Africa
Swaziland
Lesotho

Kazakhstan
Uzbekistan
Turkmenistan
Kyrgyzstan
Tajikistan
Afghanistan
Iran
Pakistan
Mongolia
China
North Korea
South Korea
Japan
Nepal
Bhutan
India
Bangladesh
Burma
Taiwan
Macao
Hong Kong
Hainan Dao
Laos
Thailand
Vietnam
Cambodia
Sri Lanka
Philippines
Brunei
Malaysia
Singapore
Indonesia
Indonesia
Papua New Guinea
Australia
New Zealand

It is estimated that the population of our planet will reach eight billion by the end of the year 2026. Many are concerned that the world's natural resources are reaching their limit in supporting so many people. Almost all of the world's population growth occurs in poorer and less developed nations, where unhealthy living conditions cause high death rates among children. High child death rates make parents want to have larger families in the hope that some of their children will survive to carry on the family name. Other causes of overpopulation in poorer countries include lack of family-planning education, and political structures that are oppressive to women. In an effort to control population growth, some governments have imposed limits on family size and mandatory sterilizations (the disabling of reproductive organs). But the more effective solutions seem to be the more democratic: education, quality health care, and programs that help impoverished women to enter social, political, and business worlds.

A n t a r c t i c a

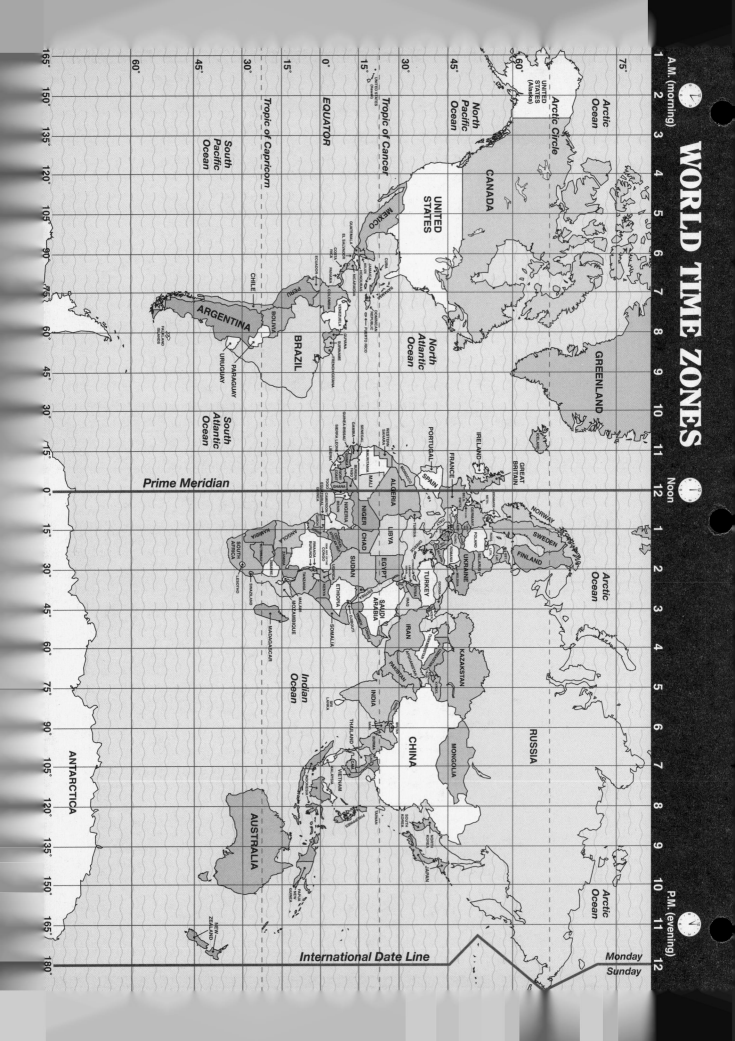

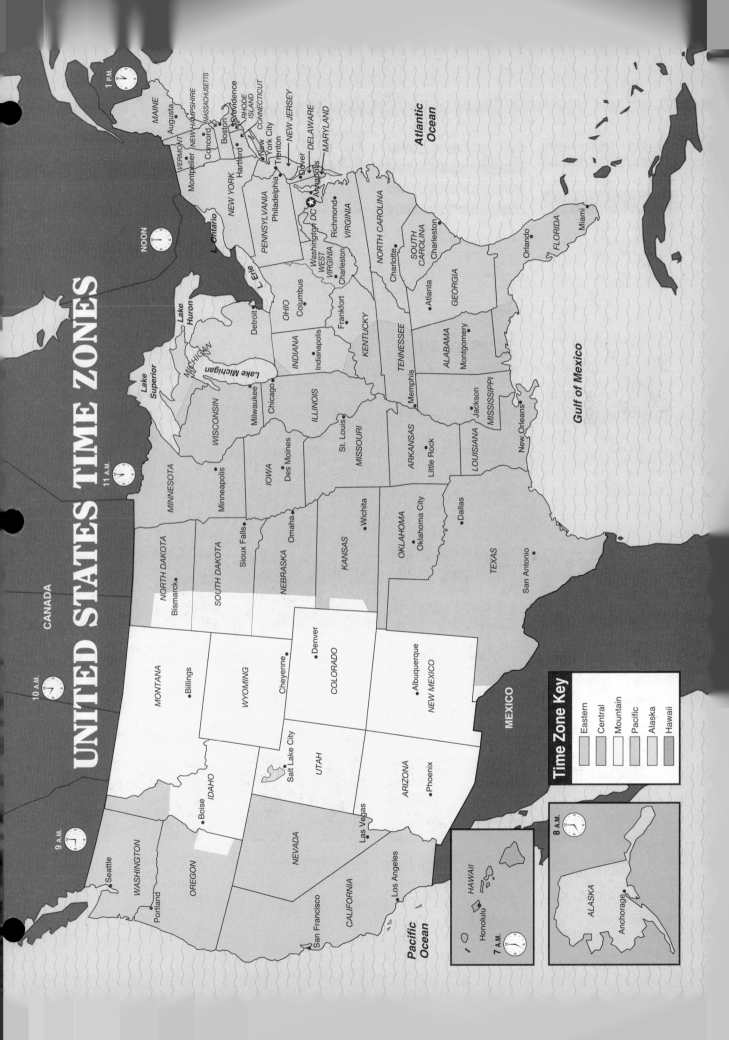

Flags of the World

Afghanistan
Capital: Kabul
Currency: afghani
Language: Afghan Persian (or Dari Persian), Pashtu, others
Location: S. Asia

Albania
Capital: Tiranë
Currency: lek
Language: Albanian, Greek
Location: E. Europe

Algeria
Capital: Algiers
Currency: Algerian dinar
Language: Arabic, Berber dialects, French
Location: N. Africa

Andorra
Capital: Andorra la Vella
Currency: euro, French franc, Spanish peseta
Language: Catalan, French, Castilian
Location: W. Europe

Angola
Capital: Luanda
Currency: kwanza
Language: Portuguese, Bantu, other African languages
Location: S. Africa

Antigua & Barbuda
Capital: St. John's
Currency: East Caribbean dollar
Language: English
Location: Caribbean Sea

Argentina
Capital: Buenos Aires
Currency: Argentine peso
Language: Spanish, English, Italian, German, French
Location: S. South America

Armenia
Capital: Yerevan
Currency: dram
Language: Armenian
Location: SW. Asia

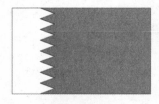

Australia
Capital: Canberra
Currency: Australian dollar
Language: English, aboriginal languages
Location: Oceania

Austria
Capital: Vienna
Currency: euro, Austrian schilling[1]
Language: German, Slovene, Croatian, Hungarian
Location: C. Europe

Azerbaijan
Capital: Baku
Currency: Azerbaijani manat
Language: Azerbaijani (Azeri), Russian, Armenian
Location: SW. Asia

Bahamas, The
Capital: Nassau
Currency: Bahamian dollar
Language: English, Creole
Location: Caribbean Sea

Bahrain
Capital: Manama
Currency: Bahrain dinar
Language: Arabic, English, Farsi, Urdu
Location: Asia (or Middle East)

Bangladesh
Capital: Dhaka
Currency: taka
Language: Bangla (Bengali), English
Location: S. Asia

Barbados
Capital: Bridgetown
Currency: Barbadian dollar
Language: English
Location: Caribbean Sea

Belarus
Capital: Minsk
Currency: Belarusian rubel
Language: Byelorussian (Belarusian), Russian
Location: E. Europe

Key: 1=former currency, 2=Communauté Financière Africaine (African Financial Community)

Flags of the World

Belgium
Capital: Brussels
Currency: euro, Belgian franc[1]
Language: Dutch, French, German
Location: W. Europe

Belize
Capital: Belmopan
Currency: Belizean dollar
Language: English, Spanish, Mayan, Garifuna (Carib), Creole
Location: Central America

Benin
Capital: Porto-Novo
Currency: CFA franc[2]
Language: French, Fon, Yoruba, other African Languages
Location: W. Africa

Bhutan
Capital: Thimphu
Currency: ngultrum, Indian rupee
Language: Dzongkha, Tibetan and Nepalese dialects
Location: S. Asia

Bolivia
Capital: Sucre and La Paz
Currency: boliviano
Language: Spanish, Quechua, Aymara
Location: C. South America

Bosnia and Herzogovina
Capital: Sarajevo
Currency: marka
Language: Croatian, Serbian, Bosnian
Location: E. Europe

Botswana
Capital: Gaborone
Currency: pula
Language: English, Setswana
Location: S. Africa

Brazil
Capital: Brasilia
Currency: real
Language: Portuguese, Spanish, English, French
Location: E. South America

Brunei
Capital: Bandar Seri Begawan
Currency: Brunei dollar
Language: Malay, English, Chinese
Location: SE. Asia

Bulgaria
Capital: Sofia
Currency: lev
Language: Bulgarian, Turkish
Location: E. Europe

Burkina Faso
Capital: Ouagadougou
Currency: CFA franc[2]
Language: French, Sudanic tribal languages
Location: W. Africa

Burundi
Capital: Bujumbura
Currency: Burundi franc
Language: Kirundi, French, Swahili
Location: C. Africa

Cambodia
Capital: Phnom Penh
Currency: riel
Language: Khmer, French, English
Location: SE. Asia

Cameroon
Capital: Yaounde
Currency: CFA franc[2]
Language: English, French, other African Languages
Location: W. Africa

Canada
Capital: Ottawa
Currency: Canadian dollar
Language: English, French
Location: N. North America

Cape Verde
Capital: Praia
Currency: Cape Verdean escudo
Language: Portuguese, Crioulo
Location: Altantic Ocean off Africa

Flags of the World

Central African Republic
Capital: Bangui
Currency: CFA franc[2]
Language: French, Sangho, Arabic, Hansa, Swahili
Location: C. Africa

Chad
Capital: N'Djamena
Currency: CFA franc[2]
Language: French, Arabic, African languages
Location: C. Africa

Chile
Capital: Santiago
Currency: Chilean peso
Language: Spanish
Location: S. South America

China, People's Republic of
Capital: Beijing
Currency: yuan
Language: Mandarin, Yue, Wu, Minbei, Minnan, Xiang, Gan, Hakka dialects, others
Location: E. Asia

Colombia
Capital: Bogotá
Currency: Colombian peso
Language: Spanish
Location: N. South America

Comoros
Capital: Moroni
Currency: Comoros franc
Language: Arabic, French, Comoran
Location: Indian Ocean off Africa

Congo, Republic of the
Capital: Brazzaville
Currency: CFA franc[2]
Language: French, Lingala, Monokutuba, Kikongo, others
Location: C. Africa

Congo, Dem. Rep. of the
Capital: Kinshasa
Currency: Congolese franc
Language: French, Bantu languages
Location: W. Africa

Costa Rica
Capital: San José
Currency: Costa Rican colón
Language: Spanish
Location: Central America

Côte d'Ivoire (Ivory Coast)
Capital: Yamoussoukro
Currency: CFA franc[2]
Language: French, Dioula, other African languages
Location: W. Africa

Croatia
Capital: Zagreb
Currency: Kuna
Language: Croatian
Location: E. Europe

Cuba
Capital: Havana
Currency: Cuban peso
Language: Spanish
Location: Caribbean Sea

Cyprus
Capital: Nicosia
Currency: Cyprus pound, Turkish lira
Language: Greek, Turkish, English
Location: Mediterranean Sea

Czech Republic
Capital: Prague
Currency: Czech koruna
Language: Czech
Location: C. Europe

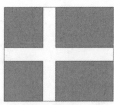

Denmark
Capital: Copenhagen
Currency: Danish krone
Language: Danish, Faroese
Location: N. Europe

Djibouti
Capital: Djibouti
Currency: Djiboutian franc
Language: Arabic, French, Afar, Somali
Location: E. Africa

Key: 1=former currency, 2=Communauté Financière Africaine (African Financial Community)

Flags of the World

Dominica
Capital: Roseau
Currency: East Caribbean dollar
Language: English, French patois
Location: Caribbean Sea

Dominican Republic
Capital: Santo Domingo
Currency: Dominican peso
Language: Spanish, English
Location: Caribbean Sea

Ecuador
Capital: Quito
Currency: U.S. dollar
Language: Spanish, Quéchua
Location: South America

Egypt
Capital: Cairo
Currency: Egyptian pound
Language: Arabic, English, French
Location: Africa

El Salvador
Capital: San Salvador
Currency: Salvadoran colón, U.S. dollar
Language: Spanish, Nahua
Location: Central America

Equatorial Guinea
Capital: Malabo
Currency: CFA franc[2]
Language: Spanish, French, pidgin English, Fang, Bubi, Ibo
Location: W. Africa

Eritrea
Capital: Asmara
Currency: nafka
Language: Tigre, Tigrinya, Afar, Amharic, Arabic, Kunama, others
Location: E. Africa

Estonia
Capital: Tallinn
Currency: Estonian kroon
Language: Estonian, Russian, Ukrainian, Finnish, English
Location: E. Europe

Ethiopia
Capital: Addis Ababa
Currency: birr
Language: Amharic, Tigrinya, Oromigna, others
Location: E. Africa

Fiji
Capital: Suva
Currency: Fijian dollar
Language: English, Fijian, Hindustani
Location: Oceania

Finland
Capital: Helsinki
Currency: euro, markka
Language: Finnish, Swedish
Location: N. Europe

France
Capital: Paris
Currency: euro, French franc
Language: French
Location: W. Europe

Gabon
Capital: Libreville
Currency: CFA franc
Language: French, Bantu languages
Location: W. Africa

Gambia, The
Capital: Banjul
Currency: dalasi
Language: English, Mandinka, Wolof, Fula
Location: W. Africa

Georgia
Capital: T'bilisi
Currency: lari
Language: Georgian, Russian
Location: S.W. Asia

Germany
Capital: Berlin
Currency: euro, Deutsche mark[1]
Language: German
Location: C. Europe

Flags of the World

Ghana
Capital: Accra
Currency: cedi
Language: English, African languages
Location: W. Africa

Greece
Capital: Athens
Currency: euro, drachma[1]
Language: Greek, English, French
Location: S. Europe

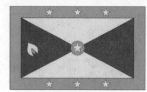

Grenada
Capital: St. George's
Currency: East Caribbean dollar
Language: English, French patois
Location: Caribbean Sea

Guatemala
Capital: Guatemala City
Currency: quetzal, U.S. dollar, others
Language: Spanish, Mayan languages
Location: Central America

Guinea
Capital: Conakry
Currency: Guinean franc
Language: French, African languages
Location: W. Africa

Guinea-Bissau
Capital: Bissau
Currency: CFA franc[2]
Language: Portuguese, Crioulo, African languages
Location: W. Africa

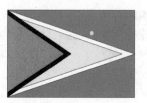

Guyana
Capital: Georgetown
Currency: Guyana dollar
Language: English, Creole, Hindi, Urdu, native South American languages
Location: N. South America

Haiti
Capital: Port-au-Prince
Currency: gourde
Language: Creole, French
Location: Caribbean Sea

Honduras
Capital: Tegucigalpa
Currency: lempira
Language: Spanish, native Central American languages
Location: Central America

Hungary
Capital: Budapest
Currency: forint
Language: Hungarian
Location: C. Europe

Iceland
Capital: Reykjavik
Currency: Icelandic krona
Language: Icelandic
Location: N. Europe

India
Capital: New Delhi
Currency: Indian rupee
Language: Hindi, English, many other languages
Location: S. Asia

Indonesia
Capital: Jakarta
Currency: Indonesian rupiah
Language: Bahasa Indonesian, Dutch, English, others
Location: SE Asia

Iran
Capital: Tehran
Currency: Iranian rial
Language: Persian, Turkic, Kurdish, others
Location: Middle East (SW. Asia)

Iraq
Capital: Baghdad
Currency: Iraqi dinar
Language: Arabic, Kurdish, Assyrian, Armenian
Location: Middle East (SW. Asia)

Ireland
Capital: Dublin
Currency: euro, Irish pound[1]
Language: English, Irish (Gaelic)
Location: W. Europe

Key: 1=former currency, 2=Communauté Financière Africaine (African Financial Community)

Flags of the World

Israel
Capital: Jerusalem
Currency: new Israeli shekel
Language: Hebrew, Arabic, English
Location: Middle East (SW. Asia)

Italy
Capital: Rome
Currency: euro, Italian lira[1]
Language: Italian, others
Location: S. Europe

Jamaica
Capital: Kingston
Currency: Jamaican dollar
Language: English, Creole
Location: Caribbean Sea

Japan
Capital: Tokyo
Currency: yen
Language: Japanese
Location: E. Asia

Jordan
Capital: Amman
Currency: Jordanian dinar
Language: Arabic, English
Location: Middle East (SW. Asia)

Kazakhstan
Capital: Astana
Currency: tenge
Language: Russian, Kazakh (or Qazaq)
Location: C. Asia

Kenya
Capital: Nairobi
Currency: Kenyan shilling
Language: English, Kiswahili, others
Location: E. Africa

Kiribati
Capital: Tarawa
Currency: Australian dollar
Language: English, I-Kiribati
Location: Oceania

Korea, North
Capital: P'yongyang
Currency: North Korean won
Language: Korean
Location: E. Asia

Korea, South
Capital: Seoul
Currency: South Korean won
Language: Korean
Location: E. Asia

Kuwait
Capital: Kuwait
Currency: Kuwaiti dinar
Language: Arabic, English
Location: Middle East (SW. Asia)

Kyrgyzstan
Capital: Bishkek
Currency: Kyrgyzstani som
Language: Kirghiz (or Kyrgyz), Russian
Location: C. Asia

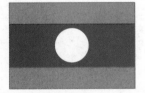

Laos
Capital: Vientiane
Currency: kip
Language: Lao, French, English
Location: SE. Asia

Latvia
Capital: Riga
Currency: Latvian lat
Language: Latvian (or Lettish), Lithuanian, Russian
Location: E. Europe

Lebanon
Capital: Beirut
Currency: Lebanese pound
Language: Arabic, French, English, Armenian
Location: Middle East (SW. Asia)

Lesotho
Capital: Maseru
Currency: loti, South African rand
Language: Sesotho, English, Zulu, Xhosa
Location: S. Africa

Flags of the World

Liberia
Capital: Monrovia
Currency: Liberian dollar
Language: English, African languages
Location: W. Africa

Libya
Capital: Tripoli
Currency: Libyan dinar
Language: Arabic, Italian, English
Location: N. Africa

Liechtenstein
Capital: Vaduz
Currency: Swiss franc
Language: German, Alemannic dialect
Location: C. Europe

Lithuania
Capital: Vilnius
Currency: litas
Language: Lithuanian, Polish, Russian
Location: E. Europe

Luxembourg
Capital: Luxembourg
Currency: euro, Luxembourg franc[1]
Language: Luxembourgish, French, German
Location: W. Europe

Macedonia
Capital: Skopje
Currency: Macedonian denar
Language: Macedonian, Albanian, others
Location: SE. Europe

Madagascar
Capital: Antananarivo
Currency: Malagasy franc
Language: Malagasy, French
Location: Indian Ocean off Africa

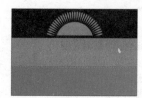

Malawi
Capital: Lilongwe
Currency: Malawian kwacha
Language: English, Chichewa
Location: S. Africa

Malaysia
Capital: Kuala Lumpur
Currency: ringgit
Language: Bahasa Melayu, Chinese, Tamil, English
Location: Asia (South Pacific)

Maldives
Capital: Malé
Currency: rufiyaa
Language: Maldivian Dhivehi
Location: Indian Ocean

Mali
Capital: Bamako
Currency: CFA franc[2]
Language: French, Bambara, other African languages
Location: W. Africa

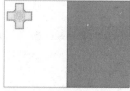

Malta
Capital: Valletta
Currency: Maltese lira
Language: Maltese, English
Location: Mediterranean Sea

Marshall Islands
Capital: Majuro
Currency: U.S. dollar
Language: English, Marshallese dialects, Japanese
Location: Oceania

Mauritania
Capital: Nouakchott
Currency: ouguiya
Language: Arabic, Wolof, French, others
Location: N. Africa

Mauritius
Capital: Port Louis
Currency: Mauritian rupee
Language: English, French, Creole, Hindi, others
Location: Indian Ocean

Mexico
Capital: Mexico City
Currency: Mexican peso
Language: Spanish, native Mexican languages
Location: S. North America

Key: 1=former currency, 2=Communauté Financière Africaine (African Financial Community)

Flags of the World

Micronesia
Capital: Palikir
Currency: U.S. dollar
Language: English, Trukese, Pohnpeian, others
Location: Oceania (South Pacific)

Moldova
Capital: Chisinau
Currency: Moldovan leu
Language: Moldovan (or Rumanian), Russian, Gagauz
Location: E. Europe

Monaco
Capital: Monaco
Currency: euro, French franc[1]
Language: French, English, Monegasque, Italian
Location: W. Europe

Mongolia
Capital: Ulaanvaator
Currency: togrog or tugrik
Language: Khalka Mongol (or Mongolian), Turkic, Russian
Location: N. Asia

Morocco
Capital: Rabat
Currency: Moroccan dirham
Language: Arabic, Berber dialects, French
Location: N. Africa

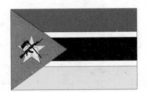

Mozambique
Capital: Maputo
Currency: metical
Language: Portuguese, native African languages
Location: Africa

Myanmar
Capital: Rangoon (Yangon)
Currency: kyat
Language: Burmese, Karen, others
Location: SE. Asia

Namibia
Capital: Windhoek
Currency: Namibian dollar, South African rand
Language: Afrikaans, English, German, native African languages
Location: S. Africa

Nauru
Capital: Yaren District
Currency: Australian dollar
Language: Nauruan, English
Location: Oceania (South Pacific)

Nepal
Capital: Kathmandu
Currency: Nepalese rupee
Language: Nepali, others
Location: S. Asia

Netherlands, The
Capital: Amsterdam
Currency: euro, Netherlands guilder[1]
Language: Dutch
Location: W. Europe

New Zealand
Capital: Wellington
Currency: New Zealand dollar
Language: English, Maori
Location: Oceania

Nicaragua
Capital: Managua
Currency: gold cordoba
Language: Spanish
Location: Central America

Niger
Capital: Niamey
Currency: CFA franc[2]
Language: French, Hausa, Djerma
Location: W. Africa

Nigeria
Capital: Abuja
Currency: naira
Language: English, Hausa, Yoruba, Igbo (Ibo), Fulani
Location: W. Africa

Norway
Capital: Oslo
Currency: Norwegian krone
Language: Norwegian
Location: N. Europe

Flags of the World

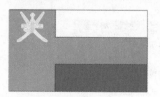

Oman
Capital: Muscat
Currency: Omani rial
Language: Arabic, others
Location: Middle East (SW Asia)

Pakistan
Capital: Islamabad
Currency: Pakistani rupee
Language: Punjabi, Sindhi, Urdu, English, others
Location: Asia

Palau, Republic of
Capital: Koror
Currency: U.S. dollar
Language: Palauan, English, others
Location: Oceania (South Pacific)

Panama
Capital: Panama City
Currency: balboa, U.S. dollar
Language: Spanish, English
Location: Central America

Papua New Guinea
Capital: Port Moresby
Currency: kina
Language: Melanesian and Papuan languages, pidgin English, English
Location: Oceania (South Pacific)

Paraguay
Capital: Asunción
Currency: guarani
Language: Spanish, Guarani
Location: C. South America

Peru
Capital: Lima
Currency: nuevo sol
Language: Spanish, Quechua, Aymara, others
Location: W. South America

Philippines
Capital: Manila
Currency: Philippine peso
Language: Filipino (based on Tagalog), English, regional languages
Location: Asia (South Pacific)

Poland
Capital: Warsaw
Currency: zloty
Language: Polish
Location: C. Europe

Portugal
Capital: Lisbon
Currency: euro, Portuguese escudo[1]
Language: Portuguese
Location: SW. Europe

Qatar
Capital: Doha
Currency: Qatari rial (or riyal)
Language: Arabic, English
Location: SW. Asia (or Middle East)

Romania
Capital: Bucharest
Currency: leu
Language: Romanian, Hungarian, German
Location: SE. Europe

Russia
Capital: Moscow
Currency: Russian ruble
Language: Russian, others
Location: N. Asia and E. Europe

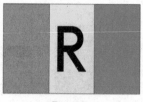

Rwanda
Capital: Kigali
Currency: Rwandan franc
Language: Kinyarwanda, French, Swahili, English
Location: C. Africa

Samoa
Capital: Apia
Currency: tala
Language: Samoan (Polynesian), English
Location: South Pacific Ocean

San Marino
Capital: San Marino
Currency: euro, Italian lira[1]
Language: Italian
Location: S. Europe

Key: 1=former currency, 2=Communauté Financière Africaine (African Financial Community)

Flags of the World

Saõ Tomé and Príncipe
Capital: Saõ Tomé
Currency: dobra
Language: Portuguese
Location: Atlantic Ocean off Africa

Saudi Arabia
Capital: Riyadh
Currency: Saudi riyal
Language: Arabic
Location: SW Asia (or Middle East)

Senegal
Capital: Dakar
Currency: CFA franc[2]
Language: French, Wolof, others
Location: W. Africa

Seychelles
Capital: Victoria
Currency: Seychelles rupee
Language: English, French, Creole
Location: Indian Ocean

Sierra Leone
Capital: Freetown
Currency: leone
Language: English, Mende, Temne, Krio
Location: W. Africa

Singapore
Capital: Singapore
Currency: Singapore dollar
Language: Malay, Chinese, Tamil, English
Location: Asia (South Pacific)

Slovakia
Capital: Bratislava
Currency: Slovak koruna
Language: Slovak, Hungarian
Location: C. Europe

Slovenia
Capital: Ljubljana
Currency: Slovenian tolar
Language: Slovenian, Serbo-Croatian
Location: SE. Europe

Solomon Islands
Capital: Honiara
Currency: Solomon Islands dollar
Language: Melanesian Pidgin, English
Location: Oceania (south Pacific)

Somalia
Capital: Mogadishu
Currency: Somali shilling
Language: Somali, Arabic, English, Italian
Location: E. Africa

South Africa
Capital: Pretoria, Cape Town, Bloemfontein
Currency: rand
Language: Afrikaans, English, Bantu languages
Location: S. Africa

Spain
Capital: Madrid
Currency: euro, Spanish peseta[1]
Language: Castilian Spanish, Catalán, Galician, Basque
Location: SW Europe

Sri Lanka
Capital: Colombo
Currency: Sri Lankan rupee
Language: Sinhala, Tamil, English
Location: Indian Ocean off India

St. Kitts and Nevis
Capital: Basseterre
Currency: East Caribbean dollar
Language: English
Location: Caribbean Sea

St. Lucia
Capital: Castries
Currency: East Caribbean dollar
Language: English, French Patois
Location: Caribbean Sea

St. Vincent and the Grenadines
Capital: Kingstown
Currency: East Caribbean dollar
Language: English, French Patois
Location: Caribbean Sea

Flags of the World

Sudan
Capital: Khartoum
Currency: Sudanese dinar
Language: Arabic, English, African tribal dialects
Location: N. Africa

Suriname
Capital: Paramaribo
Currency: Surinamese guilder
Language: Dutch, English, Sranang Tongo, Hindustani
Location: N. South America

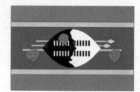

Swaziland
Capital: Mbabane
Currency: lilangeni
Language: Siswati (or siSwati), English
Location: S. Africa

Sweden
Capital: Stockholm
Currency: Swedish krona
Language: Swedish, Finnish, Lappish
Location: N. Europe

Switzerland
Capital: Bern (administrative), Lausanne (judicial)
Currency: Swiss franc
Language: German, French, Italian
Location: C. Europe

Syria
Capital: Damascus
Currency: Syrian pound
Language: Arabic, Kurdish, Armenian, others
Location: SW Asia (or Middle East)

Taiwan
Capital: Taipei
Currency: new Taiwan dollar
Language: Mandarin Chinese, Taiwanese, Hakka dialects
Location: Pacific Ocean off E. Asia

Tajikistan
Capital: Dushanbe
Currency: somoni
Language: Tajik, Russian
Location: C. Asia

Tanzania
Capital: Dar es Salaam
Currency: Tanzanian shilling
Language: Kiswahili or Swahili, English, Arabic, African languages
Location: E. Africa

Thailand
Capital: Bangkok
Currency: baht
Language: Thai, English, others
Location: SE. Asia

Togo
Capital: Lomé
Currency: CFA franc[2]
Language: French, Ewe, Mina, Kabye, Dagomba
Location: W. Africa

Tonga
Capital: Nuku'alofa
Currency: pa'anga
Language: Tongan, English
Location: Oceania (South Pacific)

Trinidad and Tobago
Capital: Port-of-Spain
Currency: Trinidad and Tobago dollar
Language: English, Hindi, others
Location: Caribbean Sea

Tunisia
Capital: Tunis
Currency: Tunisian dinar
Language: Arabic, French
Location: N. Africa

Turkey
Capital: Ankara
Currency: Turkish lira
Language: Turkish, Kurdish, Arabic
Location: SE. Europe and SW. Asia

Turkmenistan
Capital: Ashgabat
Currency: Turkmen manat
Language: Turkmen, Russian, Uzbek
Location: C. Asia

Key: 1=former currency, 2=Communauté Financière Africaine (African Financial Community)

Flags of the World

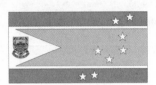

Tuvalu
Capital: Funafuti
Currency: Australian dollar, Tuvaluan dollar
Language: Tuvaluan, English
Location: Oceania (South Pacific)

Uganda
Capital: Kampala
Currency: Ugandan shilling
Language: English, Swahili, Luganda, others
Location: E. Africa

Ukraine
Capital: Kiev
Currency: hryvnia
Language: Ukrainian, Russian, others
Location: E. Europe

United Arab Emirates
Capital: Abu Dhabi
Currency: Emirati (or U.A.E.) dirham
Language: Arabic, Persian, English, Hindi, Urdu
Location: SW. Asia (or Middle East)

United Kingdom
Capital: London
Currency: British pound (or pound sterling)
Language: English, Welsh, Scottish, Gaelic
Location: W. Europe

United States of America
Capital: Washington, D.C.
Currency: U.S. dollar
Language: English, Spanish
Location: North America

Uruguay
Capital: Montevideo
Currency: Uruguayan peso
Language: Spanish, Portunol, Brazilero
Location: S. South America

Uzbekistan
Capital: Tashkent
Currency: Uzbekistani sum
Language: Uzbek, Russian
Location: C. Asia

Vanuatu
Capital: Port-Vila
Currency: vatu
Language: English, French, pidgin (Bislama)
Location: Oceania (South Pacific)

Vatican City
Capital: Vatican City
Currency: euro, Vatican lira
Language: Latin, Italian, others
Location: S. Europe

Venezuela
Capital: Caracas
Currency: bolivar
Language: Spanish, native South American languages
Location: N. South America

Vietnam
Capital: Hanoi
Currency: dong
Language: Vietnamese, French, English, Khmer, Chinese
Location: SE. Asia

Yemen
Capital: Sanaá
Currency: Yemeni rial
Language: Arabic
Location: SW. Asia (or Middle East)

Yugoslavia
Capital: Belgrade
Currency: new Yugoslav dinar
Language: Serbian
Location: SE. Europe

Zambia
Capital: Lusaka
Currency: Zambian kwacha
Language: English, Bantu languages
Location: S. Africa

Zimbabwe
Capital: Harare
Currency: Zimbabwean dollar
Language: English, Sindebele, Shona
Location: S. Africa

World Explorers

TRAVELER	FROM	DISCOVERY	DISTANCE	DATE	MODE	TIME
Marco Polo	Venice, Italy	Shangdu, China	7,500 miles	1271–1274	boat and camel	3 years
Christopher Columbus	Spain	West Indies	4,500 miles	1492	caravel	2 months, 9 days
Giovani Caboto (John Cabot)	Britain	North American mainland	500 miles	1497	small caravel	33 days
Vasco da Gama	Lisbon, Portugal	India	12,000 miles	1497–1498	caravel	10 months
Amerigo Vespucci	Portugal	South America	6,000 miles of coast	1501	caravel	3 months
Vasco Nunez de Balboa	Hispaniola	Pacific Ocean	1,000 miles	1513	two-masted sailing ship	32 days
Ponce de Leon	Spain	Florida	1,100 miles	1513	caravel	24 days
Hernando Cortes	Cuba	Mexico	1,600 miles	1519	caravel	35 days
Ferdinand Magellan	Spain	sailed around South America and back to Spain	50,000 miles	1519–1521	caravel	3 years
Jacques Cartier	France	St. Lawrence River	5,000 mles	1535	three caravels	2 months, 23 days
Francisco Coronado	Spain	Southwest U.S.	3,300 miles	1540–1542	foot; horseback	2 years
Samuel de Champlain	France	Maine coast	5,500 miles	1604–1607	caravel	3 years

TRAVELER	FROM	DISCOVERY	DISTANCE	DATE	MODE	TIME
Robert Fulton	United States	Albany, NY	150 miles	1807	steamboat	30 hours
Nathaniel Palmer & Fabian Gottlieb Von Bellingshausen	United States & Russia	Antarctica	700 miles from the tip of South America	1820–1821	sloop (small vessel with triangular sails)	2 years
Robert E. Peary	United States	North Pole	450 miles	1909	dog sled	31 days
Calbraith Rodgers	United States	New York to California	3,000 miles	1911	airplane	84 days
Charles Lindbergh	United States	New York to Paris	3,610 miles	1927	airplane	33 1/2 hours
Amelia Earhart	United States	first woman to fly solo across Atlantic Ocean	2,026 miles	1932	airplane	15 hours
Yuri Gagarin	Soviet Union	First human in space	1 orbit of Earth, 203 miles above	1961	Vostok rocket	89 minutes
Neil Armstrong & Edward Aldrin	United States	First humans to walk on the moon	215,000 miles from Earth	1969	spacecraft and lunar module	4 days
Clay Lacy	United States	Flew around the world	26,345 miles	1988	airplane	37 hours
Shannon Lucid	United States	first woman to spend extended time in space	240 miles above Earth	1996	space shuttle and space station	6 months
ordinary citizens	the world	flight from New York, NY to London	3,469 miles	1996	supersonic transport	3 hours

Sources: *World Explorers and Discoverers*, Richard E. Bohlander, editor, 1992.; *Explorers and Discoverers of the World*, Daniel B. Baker, editor, 1993.

Provinces and Territories of Canada

Alberta
Capital: Edmonton
Entered Confederation: September 1, 1905

•Home of the annual Calgary stampede.
•Land mass nearly equal to that of Texas.

British Columbia
Capital: Victoria
Entered Confederation: July 20, 1871

•Vancouver cited as teh most "livable city in the world" by the United Nations.

Manitoba
Capital: Winnipeg
Entered Confederation: July 15, 1870

•One of the largest Mennonite populations in the world.

New Brunswick
Capital: Fredericton
Entered Confederation: July 1, 1867

•Land is 85% forest.
•Highest percentage of French speakers outside of Quebec.

Newfoundland and Labrador
Capital: St. John's
Entered Confederation: March 31, 1949

•John Cabot claimed "St. John's Isle" in 1497 for Henry VII of England.

Northwest Territories
Capital: Yellowknife
Entered Confederation: July 15, 1870

•Located above the 60th parallel.
•Eight official languages.

Nova Scotia
Capital: Halifax
Entered Confederation: July 1, 1867

•Halifax explosion of 1917 was the deadliest man-made explosion prior to the atomic bomb.

Nunavut
Capital: Iqualit
Entered Confederation: April 1, 1999

•Canada's newest territory, established in 1999.
•Population primarily Inuit.

Ontario
Capital: Toronto
Entered Confederation: July 1, 1867

•First province to enter confederation.
•Most populous province in Canada.

Prince Edward Island
Capital: Charlottetown
Entered Confederation: July 1, 1873

•Smallest province in area.
•Best known for *Anne of Green Gables* by Lucy Maud Montogmery.

Quebec
Capital: Quebec
Entered Confederation: July 1, 1867

•French is the main spoken language.
•Largest province in area.

Saskatchewan
Capital: Regina
Entered Confederation: September 1, 1905

•Elected the first socialist government in North America in 1944.

Yukon Territory
Capital: Whitehorse
Entered Confederation: June 13, 1898

•Experienced Klondike Gold Rush in the late 1800's

Sir John Alexander Macdonald

Born: January 11, 1815
In office: 1867-1873, 1878-1891
Party: Liberal Conservative
Died: June 6, 1891

Alexander Mackenzie

Born: January 28, 1822
In office: 1873-1878
Party: Liberal
Died: April 17, 1892

Sir John Joseph Caldwell Abbott

Born: March 12, 1821
In office: 1891-1892
Party: Liberal Conservative
Died: October 30, 1893

Sir John Sparrow David Thompson

Born: November 10, 1845
In office: 1892-1894
Party: Liberal Conservative
Died: December 12, 1894

Sir Mackenzie Bowell

Born: December 17, 1823
In office: 1894-1896
Party: Liberal Conservative
Died: December 10, 1917

Sir Charles Tupper

Born: July 2, 1821
In office: 1896
Party: Conservative
Died: October 30, 1915

Sir Wilfrid Laurier

Born: November 20, 1841
In office: 1896-1911
Party: Liberal
Died: February 17, 1919

Sir Robert Laird Borden

Born: June 26, 1854
In office: 1911-1917, 1917-1920
Party: Conservative
Died: June 10, 1937

Arthur Meighen

Born: June 16, 1874
In office: 1920-1921, 1926
Party: Conservative
Died: August 5, 1960

William Lyon Mackenzie King

Born: December 17, 1874
In office: 1921-1926, 1926-1930, 1935-1947
Party: Liberal
Died: July 22, 1950

Richard Bedford Bennett

Born: July 3, 1870
In office: 1930-1935
Party: Conservative
Died: June 26, 1947

Louis Stephen St-Laurent

Born: February 1, 1882
In office: 1948-1957
Party: Liberal
Died: July 25, 1973

John George Diefenbaker

Born: September 18, 1895
In office: 1957-1963
Party: Progressive Conservative
Died: August 16, 1979

Lester Bowles Pearson

Born: April 23, 1897
In office: 1963-1968
Party: Liberal
Died: December 27, 1972

Pierre Elliott Trudeau

Born: October 18, 1919
In office: 1968 to 1979, 1980 to 1984
Party: Liberal
Died: September 28, 2000

Charles Joseph Clark

Born: June 5, 1939
In office: 1979-1980
Party: Progressive Conservative

John Napier Turner

Born: June 7, 1929
In office: 1984
Party: Liberal

Martin Brian Mulroney

Born: March 20, 1939
In office: 1984-1993
Party: Progressive Conservative

Kim Campbell

Born: March 10, 1947
In office: 1993
Party: Progressive Conservative

Jean Chrétien

Born: January 11, 1934
In office: 1993 to Present
Party: Liberal

European Languages and Religions

Language	The majority of people in present-day Europe speak a language from one of three language subgroups in the Indo-European language family. These language subgroups are Romance, Germanic, and Slavic.		

Romance	Germanic	Slavic
Spanish	German	Polish
Portuguese	English	Czech
French	Dutch	Slovak
Italian	Norwegian	Ukrainian
Romanian	Swedish	Russian

Religion	The majority of people in Europe are Christians, usually Roman Catholic, Protestant, or Eastern Orthodox.		

Roman Catholic	Protestant	Eastern Orthodox
Spain	northern Germany	Greece
Portugal	Great Britain	Bulgaria
France	the Netherlands	Romania
Italy	Norway	Serbia
Belgium	Sweden	Ukraine
Ireland	Denmark	Russia
	Iceland	
large parts of:	Finland	
the Netherlands	Poland	
Germany		
Austria		
Poland		
Hungary		
Czechoslovakia		

Judaism, a non-Christian religion, is represented by small groups of people throughout Europe. Islam, another non-Christian religion, is represented in small areas in Albania and others parts of the Balkan Peninsula (which includes Croatia and Bosnia).

Countries in which Arabic Is the Main Language

1. Algeria
2. Bahrain
3. Chad
4. Comoros
5. Djibouti
6. Egypt
7. Iraq
8. Jordan
9. Kuwait
10. Lebanon
11. Libya
12. Mauritania
13. Morocco
14. Oman
15. Qatar
16. Saudi Arabia
17. Somalia
18. Sudan
19. Syria
20. Tunisia
21. United Arab Emirates
22. Yemen

Countries in which Islam Is the Main Religion

1. Afghanistan
2. Algeria
3. Azerbaijan
4. Bahrain
5. Bangladesh
6. Brunei
7. Chad
8. Comoros
9. Djibouti
10. Egypt
11. Gambia
12. Guinea
13. Guinea-Bissau
14. Indonesia
15. Iran
16. Iraq
17. Jordan
18. Kyrgyzstan
19. Kuwait
20. Kazakhstan
21. Lebanon
22. Libya
23. Malaysia
24. Maldives
25. Mali
26. Mauritania
27. Morocco
28. Niger
29. Nigeria
30. Oman
31. Pakistan
32. Qatar
33. Saudi Arabia
34. Senegal
35. Somalia
36. Sudan
37. Syria
38. Tajikistan
39. Tunisia
40. Turkey
41. Turkmenistan
42. United Arab Emirates
43. Uzbekistan
44. Western Sahara
45. Yemen

Source: *Planet Earth*, Jill Bailey and Catherine Thompson, 1993

Asian Languages and Religions

Language	Though English is spoken in parts of Asia, there are many languages that are unrelated to those spoken in Europe. Asian languages are derived from different language families.
	The two main language families are Altaic and Sino-Tibetan. Within each of these language families are several language subgroups. The presence of so many different languages from different families and subgroups makes it difficult to put the languages into broad categories like we did for Europe.
Religion	Christian religions are practiced in some parts of Asia, but the majority of Asians practice non-Christian religions. These include Buddism, Hinduism, Islam, traditional faiths, and tribal religions.

Buddhism	Hinduism	Islam

Myanmar
Thailand
Cambodia
Laos
Tibet
Mongolia
	India
	Nepal
	Bhutan
	Sri Lanka
	Singapore
		Pakistan
		Bangladesh
		Afghanistan
		Saudi Arabia
		Iraq
		Iran
		
		parts of:
		    China
		    the former Soviet Union

Traditional faiths and tribal religions, which are based on ancient, community beliefs, are practiced mostly in northern and eastern Asia, and in parts of Saudia Arabia.

Sources: *Geography: Realms, Religions, and Concepts*, H.J. de Blij and Peter O. Muller, 1994; *The Cambridge Encyclopedia of Languages*, David Crystal, 1994; *Human Geography: Landscapes of Human Activity*, J. Fellmann, A. Getis, and J. Getis, 1992

Major Straits of the World

Strait	Size	Control	History
Dardanelles (Sea of Marmara to the Aegean Sea)	5 miles wide; 1 mile wide at its narrowest point; 38 miles long; 200 feet deep	Turkey	This strait controls access to the cities northeast of Turkey. It has been of great strategic and economic importance throughout history. During World War I Allied fleets attempted to take control of the strait. The Turks held the Allies off, securing control of the area.
Bosporus (Black Sea to the Sea of Marmara)	2.3 miles wide; 800 yards wide at its narrowest point; 19 miles long	Turkey	Pressure from Russia and Europe resulted in several treaties, leading to the Montreux Convention of 1936. Turkey was granted full control of the strait.
Hormuz (Persian Gulf to the Gulf of Oman)	40–60 miles wide	No country has been given control of the strait.	This strait is an important petroleum shipping route from the oil-producing countries of southwest Asia.
Gibraltar (Atlantic Ocean to the Mediterranean Sea)	8–23 miles wide; 32 miles long; 1,050 feet deep at its shallowest point	No country has been given control of the strait.	Control of this strategic strait has long been valued because it permits entry into the Mediterranean, and therefore, access to Europe, Asia, and Africa. The strait is also important because as surface water moves east from the Atlantic, the deeper water moves west toward the Atlantic. This movement helps circulate the Mediterranean Sea.
Suez Canal* (Mediterranean Sea to the Red Sea) * Functions like a strait; is really an isthmus	741 feet wide at surface and 302 wide at the bottom; 118 miles long; 64 feet deep	Egypt	In 1858 France and Egypt agreed to build a maritime canal, creating the Suez Canal Company which was to operate the canal for 99 years. In 1875 Britain bought out Egypt's share of the canal. In 1956 Egypt took control of the company and seized all of its Egyptian assets.

Source: *World Book Encyclopedia,* 1991;
National Geographic Exploring Your World, 1993; *National Geographic Picture Atlas of Our World,* 1993

Hurricanes, Typhoons, and Cyclones

A hurricane is a storm with violent winds of more than 75 miles per hour circulating around a calm center. Hurricanes are usually accompanied by heavy rains, high tides, and floods, in regions along the coasts.

This type of storm is called a hurricane when it occurs in the eastern Pacific and Atlantic Oceans, a typhoon when it occurs in the China Sea and the western Pacific Ocean, and a tropical cyclone when it occurs in the Indian Ocean. Winds circulate in a counterclockwise direction in the northern hemisphere, and clockwise in the southern hemisphere.

Hurricanes, typhoons, and cyclones form over warm tropical and subtropical waters during the time of year when water temperatures are the warmest, and humidity is the highest. These storms form when an easterly wave, an area of low pressure, deepens and intensifies. The warm water and air over these low pressure areas create instability. Winds begin circulating and the storm moves westward, growing stronger and larger. Some hurricanes measure 200–300 miles across. Winds swirl around an eye, a 20-mile diameter calm spot in the center of the storm. Wall clouds are clouds surrounding the eye. They contain the strongest winds and heaviest rain.

Hurricane winds can reach speeds of 130 to 150 miles per hour. High speed winds, combined with the force of the ocean produce huge waves called storm surges, which cause flooding. Heavy rainfall caused by the storm also causes flooding.

The Kalahari Desert

The Kalahari Desert is not considered a true desert by some scientists who claim that a true desert receives less than ten inches of rain per year. Many scientists argue that the Kalahari is a semidesert since it receives as much as 15 inches of rainfall per year in some places. Scientists say that it is not the lack of rainfall that makes this area a desert. Instead, they explain that the sandy soils and lack of surface water, such as rivers and lakes, are the reasons for the lack of lush vegetation.

Month	Average Monthly Rainfall (inches)
January	4.2
February	3.1
March	2.8
April	0.7
May	0.2
June	0.1
July	0
August	0
September	0
October	0.9
November	2.2
December	3.4

The Sahara Desert

The Sahara Desert stretches across northern Africa and covers parts of ten countries, making it the world's largest desert. It is also the world's driest desert. Almost all parts of the Sahara receive less than ten inches of rainfall each year, making it barren.

Month	Average Monthly Rainfall (inches)
January	0.1
February	0.1
March	0
April	0
May	0
June	0
July	0.1
August	0
September	0
October	0
November	0.2
December	0.1

Sources: *World Weather Guide*, E.A. Pearce and Gordon Smith, 1990; *Grolier Electronic Encyclopedia*, 1995

Desert Data

What Causes Deserts to Form

Physical Location

- location between 15° and 30° north and south of the equator
- distance from available water such as lakes and oceans
- rain shadows – areas sheltered from the prevailing winds by a mountain range; rain falls on one side of the mountain, but not on the other

Climate Patterns

- circulation of air from the equator to the poles that produces high pressure areas that prevent moisture from entering
- cold ocean currents that cool water and prevent evaporation
- prevailing winds that carry dry air over the area

Human Activity

- existing plant life lost through poor agricultural practices, overgrazing, and the cutting of trees for fuel or to create more cropland
- mining that strips the land and contaminates the water
- inefficient water management
- deep wells that deplete fossil water which cannot be replaced

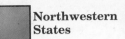 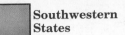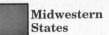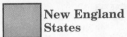
Alabama

Capital: Montgomery
Population: 4,283,000
Size: 51,705 sq. miles

Statehood: December 14, 1819
State Bird: Yellowhammer
State Flower: Camellia
Nickname: The Heart of Dixie
State Postal Abbreviation: AL

Famous Natives: Helen Keller (author, educator), Rosa Parks (civil rights activist), Jesse Owens (athlete), Harper Lee (author)

State Greats: Russell Cave, Tuskegee Institute

Fun Facts:
• World's first electric streetcars ran in the U.S. (Montgomery, 1886)
• Civil rights movement began when Rosa Parks refused to give up her seat on a bus for a white person (Montgomery, 1955)
• Home to the first capital of the Confederate States of America

22nd state

Alaska

Capital: Juneau
Population: 551,947
Size: 591,004 sq. miles

Statehood: January 3, 1959
State Bird: Willow Ptarmigan
State Flower: Forget-Me-Not
Nickname: The Last Frontier
State Postal Abbreviation: AK

Famous Natives: William Egan (first state governor), Benny Benson (designer of state flag), Carl Ben Eielson (pioneer pilot), Joe Juneau (prospector)

State Greats: Mount McKinley, Point Barrow

Fun Facts:
• Largest state in the U.S.
• Only 50 miles from Russia at the westernmost point
• Called "Seward's Folly" because many people thought Secretary of State William Seward wasted money purchasing it (he gave Russia $7,200,000 in 1867)
• Home of Mt. McKinley, the highest point in North America

49th state

Arizona

Capital: Phoenix
Population: 3,677,985
Size: 114,000 sq. miles

Statehood: February 14, 1912
State Bird: Cactus Wren
State Flower: Saguaro Blossom
Nickname: The Grand Canyon State
State Postal Abbreviation: AZ

Famous Natives: Geronimo (Apache Indian chief), Sandra Day O'Connor (first woman U.S. Supreme Court justice), Frank Luke, Jr. (World War II fighter ace), Cesar Estrada Chavez (labor leader)

State Greats: Grand Canyon, Hoover Dam, Meteor Crater

Fun Facts:
• Location of the first organized rodeo (1888)
• Original London Bridge relocated and reassembled piece by piece
• Home of Grand Canyon National Park
• Home of Kitts Peak National Observatory where the world's largest solar telescope is located

48th state

Arkansas

Capital: Little Rock
Population: 2,473,000
Size: 53,187 sq. miles

Statehood: June 15, 1836
State Bird: Mockingbird
State Flower: Apple Blossom
Nickname: The Land of Opportunity
State Postal Abbreviation: AR

Famous Natives: William Jefferson Clinton (U.S. president), Maya Angelou (author and poet), Douglas MacArthur (5-star general)

State Greats: Hot Springs, Crater of Diamonds State Park

Fun Facts:
• Part of the Louisiana Purchase
• Explored by Hernando De Soto (1541)
• Bordered by the Mississippi River to the east
• Home of Ouachita National Forest, the oldest national forest in the south

25th state

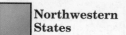
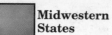

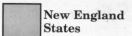
California

Capital: Sacramento
Population: 29,839,250
Size: 158,706 sq. miles

Statehood: September 9, 1850
State Bird: California Valley Quail
State Flower: Golden Poppy
Nickname: The Golden State
State Postal Abbreviation: CA

Famous Natives: Shirley Temple Black (actress, ambassador), Robert Frost (poet), Sally Ride (astronaut), George S. Patton, Jr. (general)

State Greats: Disneyland, Sequoia National Park, Death Valley

Fun Facts:
- Most heavily populated state
- Home to the world's largest living trees (Sequoia National Park)
- Belonged to Mexico until 1848
- First motion picture theater opened (Los Angeles, 1902)

31st state

Colorado

Capital: Denver
Population: 3,307,912
Size: 104,091 sq. miles

Statehood: August 1, 1876
State Bird: Lark Bunting
State Flower: Rocky Mountain Columbine
Nickname: The Centennial State
State Postal Abbreviation: CO

Famous Natives: Kit Carson (frontiersman), Patricia Schroeder (politician), Jack Dempsey (boxer), Ben Nighthorse Campbell (senator)

State Greats: Pikes Peak, Dinosaur National Monument

Fun Facts:
- Anasazi peoples built pueblo villages at Mesa Verde around 750 A.D.
- Highest average elevation of any state
- Location of the world's highest suspension bridge (Royal Gorge Bridge)
- Katherine Lee Bates was inspired to write the song "America the Beautiful" after a visit to Pikes Peak

38th state

Connecticut

Capital: Hartford
Population: 3,296,000
Size: 5,018 sq. miles

Statehood: January 9, 1788
State Bird: Robin
State Flower: Mountain Laurel
Nickname: The Constitution State
State Postal Abbreviation: CT

Famous Natives: Ethan Allan (American Revolutionary soldier), Harriet Beecher Stowe (author), P.T. Barnum (showman), Frederick Law Olmsted (landscape designer)

State Greats: U.S.S. Nautilus, Yale University

Fun Facts:
- State song is "Yankee Doodle"
- Birthplace of mass production manufacturing (1808)
- Home of Scoville Memorial Library, the oldest public library in the U.S. (1771)
- Hartford Courant is the oldest newspaper in the U.S., first printed in 1764

5th state

Delaware

Capital: Dover
Population: 669,000
Size: 2,045 sq. miles

Statehood: December 7, 1787
State Bird: Blue Hen Chicken
State Flower: Peach Blossom
Nickname: The First State
State Postal Abbreviation: DE

Famous Natives: Henry Heimlich (surgeon, inventor), E. I. du Pont (industrialist), Annie Jump Cannon (astronomer), George Read (jurist, signer of The Declaration of Independence)

State Greats: Holy Trinity Church—oldest Protestant church in U.S. still in use, New Castle historic district

Fun Facts:
- First state to join the Union
- Named after Thomas West, known as "Lord de la Warr", the first governor of Virginia
- First state to ratify the U.S. Constitution
- Nylon first produced at DuPont Laboratories, making the state the nylon capital of the world

1st state

Florida

Capital: Tallahassee
Population: 13,003,362
Size: 58,664 sq. miles

Statehood: March 3, 1845
State Bird: Mockingbird
State Flower: Orange Blossom
Nickname: The Sunshine State
State Postal Abbreviation: FL

Famous Natives: Mary McLeod Bethune (educator), Chris Evert (tennis player), Osceola (Seminole Indian chief), Janet Reno (attorney general)

State Greats: Kennedy Space Center, Disney World, Everglades

Fun Facts:
- Theme park capital of the world
- Name Florida comes from a Spanish word meaning "feast of flowers"
- Location of Saint Augustine, the oldest city in the U.S. (1565)
- Site of Cape Canaveral

27th state

Georgia

Capital: Atlanta
Population: 7,184,000
Size: 58,910 sq. miles

Statehood: January 2, 1788
State Bird: Brown Thrasher
State Flower: Cherokee Rose
Nickname: The Peach State
State Postal Abbreviation: GA

Famous Natives: Jimmy Carter (U.S. president), Martin Luther King, Jr. (civil rights activist), Juliette Gordon Low (U.S. Girl Scouts founder), Margaret Mitchell (author)

State Greats: Largest state east of the Mississippi River, Fort Benning

Fun Facts:
- Girl Scouts organization began
- Coca-Cola® was invented
- Leading producer of peaches, peanuts, and pecans in the U.S.
- Wesleyan College in Macon was the first college in the world to grant degrees to women

4th state

Hawaii

Capital: Honolulu
Population: 1,243,000
Size: 6,471 sq. miles

Statehood: August 21, 1959
State Bird: Nene (Hawaiian Goose)
State Flower: Hibiscus
Nickname: The Aloha State
State Postal Abbreviation: HI

Famous Natives: King Kamehameha I (first Hawaiian king), Queen Liliuokalani (last Hawaiian monarch), Hiram Fong (first Asian-American senator)

State Greats: Pearl Harbor, Diamond Head

Fun Facts:
- Only state made up entirely of islands
- Home to the Haleakala Crater, the world's largest dormant volcano
- Sport of surfing invented here
- Iolani Palace - only royal palace in the U.S., located on the Big Island of Hawaii

50th state

Idaho

Capital: Boise
Population: 1,164,000
Size: 83,564 sq. miles

Statehood: July 3, 1890
State Bird: Mountain Bluebird
State Flower: Syringa
Nickname: The Gem State
State Postal Abbreviation: ID

Famous Natives: Sacajawea (Shoshone Indian, interpreter), Ezra Pound (poet), Gutzon Borglum (Mt. Rushmore sculptor), J.R. Simplot (industrialist)

State Greats: Snake River Birds of Prey Natural Area, Hell's Canyon

Fun Facts:
- Leading producer of silver in the U.S.
- Explored by Lewis and Clark (1805)
- Television invented here
- Home of Soda Springs, the largest man-made geyser in the world

43rd state

Illinois

21st state

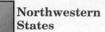

Capital: Springfield
Population: 11,467,000
Size: 56,345 sq. miles

Statehood: December 3, 1818
State Bird: Cardinal
State Flower: Native Violet
Nickname: The Prairie State
State Postal Abbreviation: IL

Famous Natives: Black Hawk (Sauk Indian chief), Frank Lloyd Wright (architect), Walt Disney (film animator, producer), Wild Bill Hickok (scout)

State Greats: Sears Tower, first Ferris Wheel

Fun Facts:
- Abraham Lincoln's home for most of his life
- Home of the world's first skyscraper (Chicago, 1885)
- First state to ratify 13th amendment to the U.S. Constitution which abolished slavery (1865)
- Home of the Chicago Public Library, the world's largest public library with over 2 million books

Indiana

19th state

Capital: Indianapolis
Population: 5,841,000
Size: 36,185 sq. miles

Statehood: December 11, 1816
State Bird: Cardinal
State Flower: Peony
Nickname: The Hoosier State
State Postal Abbreviation: IN

Famous Natives: William Henry Harrison (U.S. president), Larry Bird (basketball player), James Dean (actor), Sarah Walker, "Madame J.C." (cosmetics entrepreneur, one of nation's first women millionaires)

State Greats: Indianapolis 500

Fun Facts:
- Raggedy Ann doll created (1914)
- Explored by Rene-Robert Cavalier sierur de La Salle (1673)
- First professional baseball game played here (Fort Wayne, 1871)
- Indianapolis Motor Speedway - site of the first long distance auto race (1911)

Iowa

29th state

Capital: Des Moines
Population: 2,865,000
Size: 56,275 sq. miles

Statehood: December 28, 1846
State Bird: Eastern Goldfinch
State Flower: Wild Rose
Nickname: The Hawkeye State
State Postal Abbreviation: IA

Famous Natives: William Buffalo Bill Cody (scout), John Wayne (actor), Herbert Hoover (U.S. president), Mamie Doud Eisenhower (presidential first lady)

State Greats: Effigy Mounds National Monument, Grant Wood Museum

Fun Facts:
- Only state name that starts with two vowels
- Once completely covered by glaciers
- Leading producer of hogs and corn in the U.S.
- Only state bordered on both east and west by water (the Mississippi River on the east, the Missouri River on the west)

Kansas

34th state

Capital: Topeka
Population: 2,591,000
Size: 82,277 sq. miles

Statehood: January 29, 1861
State Bird: Western Meadowlark
State Flower: Sunflower
Nickname: The Sunflower State
State Postal Abbreviation: KS

Famous Natives: Amelia Earhart (aviator), Walter P. Chrysler (auto manufacturer), Barry Sanders (football player), Susan Madora Salter (first woman mayor in the U.S.)

State Greats: Agricultural Hall of Fame, Kansas Cosmosphere and Space Center, Boot Hill

Fun Facts:
- Geographic center of the 48 contiguous states
- Leading producer of wheat in the U.S.
- Part of the Dust Bowl during the 1930s
- Largest population of wild grouse (prairie chickens) in North America

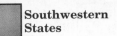

Kentucky

Capital: Frankfort
Population: 3,864,000
Size: 40,410 sq. miles

Statehood: June 1, 1792
State Bird: Cardinal
State Flower: Goldenrod
Nickname: The Bluegrass State
State Postal Abbreviation: KY

Famous Natives: Abraham Lincoln (U.S. president), Jefferson Davis (president of the Confederacy), Carry Amelia Nation (temperance leader), Muhammad Ali (boxer)

State Greats: Kentucky Derby, Mammoth Cave National Park, Fort Knox

Fun Facts:
- Home to Cumberland Gap, an important passageway for early pioneers
- Sided with the Union during the Civil War, although it is a southern state
- Leading producer of bituminous coal in the U.S.
- Site of the world's largest cave (Mammoth Cave)

15th state

Louisiana

Capital: Baton Rouge
Population: 4,389,000
Size: 47,472 sq. miles

Statehood: April 30, 1812
State Bird: Brown Pelican
State Flower: Magnolia
Nickname: The Pelican State
State Postal Abbreviation: LA

Famous Natives: Truman Capote (author), Louis Armstrong (musician), Michael De Bakey (heart surgeon), Huey P. Long (politician)

State Greats: Mardi Gras, Mississippi Delta

Fun Facts:
- Produces 90 percent of all crayfish in the U.S.
- Site of the final battles of the War of 1812
- Claimed for France by the explorer, Rene-Robert Cavelier sierur de La Salle (1682)
- Site of the tallest state capital building in the U.S.

18th state

Maine

Capital: Augusta
Population: 1,245,000
Size: 33,265 sq. miles

Statehood: March 15, 1820
State Bird: Chickadee
State Flower: White Pine Cone and Tassel
Nickname: The Pine Tree State
State Postal Abbreviation: ME

Famous Natives: Henry Wadsworth Longfellow (poet), Margaret Chase Smith (politician), Stephen King (author), Dorothea Dix (civil rights reformer)

State Greats: Acadia National Park, lobsters, Kennebunkport

Fun Facts:
- Only state that shares a border with only one other state
- Probably visited by Leif Ericson, a Viking, around 1000 A.D.
- Largest single producer of blueberries in the U.S.
- Site of the first sawmill in the U.S. (1623)

23rd state

Maryland

Capital: Annapolis
Population: 5,105,000
Size: 10,460 sq. miles

Statehood: April 28, 1788
State Bird: Baltimore Oriole
State Flower: Black-Eyed Susan
Nickname: The Old Line State
State Postal Abbreviation: MD

Famous Natives: Frederick Douglass (abolitionist), Harriet Tubman (abolitionist), Babe Ruth (baseball player), Francis Scott Key (lawyer, author)

State Greats: U.S. Naval Academy

Fun Facts:
- Explored by Captain John Smith (1608)
- Almost cut in half by the Chesapeake Bay
- Francis Scott Key, a Maryland lawyer, wrote the "Star Spangled Banner" (1818)
- Site of King Williams School, the first school in the U.S. (1696)

7th state

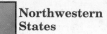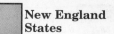
Massachusetts

Capital: Boston
Population: 6,062,000
Size: 8,284 sq. miles

Statehood: February 6, 1788
State Bird: Chickadee
State Flower: Mayflower
Nickname: The Bay State
State Postal Abbreviation: MA

Famous Natives: Susan B. Anthony (woman suffragist), Emily Dickinson (poet), John F. Kennedy (U.S. president), John Hancock (statesman)

State Greats: Harvard University, Cape Cod

Fun Facts:
- Location of the famous Salem witchcraft trials (1692)
- Location of Plymouth, where the Pilgrims landed (1620) and later celebrated the first Thanksgiving (1621)
- Minutemen fought the British at Lexington and Concord, beginning the Revolutionary War (1775)
- Location of the Basketball Hall of Fame, Springfield

6th state

Michigan

Capital: Lansing
Population: 9,654,000
Size: 58,527 sq. miles

Statehood: January 26, 1837
State Bird: Robin
State Flower: Apple Blossom
Nickname: The Wolverine State
State Postal Abbreviation: MI

Famous Natives: Charles Lindbergh (aviator), Henry Ford (industrialist), Roger Chaffee (astronaut), Gerald R. Ford (U.S. president)

State Greats: Detroit—known as the "Motor City," Greenfield Village

Fun Facts:
- Shares a border with Canada
- Also known as "The Great Lakes State", it is the only state that touches four of the five Great Lakes
- Battle Creek is known as the cereal capital of the world
- Detroit is known as the car capital of the world

26th state

Minnesota

Capital: St. Paul
Population: 4,642,000
Size: 84,402 sq. miles

Statehood: May 11, 1858
State Bird: Common Loon
State Flower: Lady's Slipper
Nickname: The Gopher State
State Postal Abbreviation: MN

Famous Natives: F. Scott Fitzgerald (author), Sinclair Lewis (author), Roger Maris (baseball player), Charles Horace Mayo and William J. Mayo (surgeons)

State Greats: Mayo Clinic, Mall of America

Fun Facts:
- Known as the "Land of 10,000 Lakes"
- Location of the northernmost point in the continental U.S.
- Said to have been the home of the tall tale hero, Paul Bunyan
- First open heart surgery performed at the Medical School of the University of Minnesota

32nd state

Mississippi

Capital: Jackson
Population: 2,676,000
Size: 47,689 sq. miles

Statehood: December 10, 1817
State Bird: Mockingbird
State Flower: Magnolia
Nickname: The Magnolia State
State Postal Abbreviation: MS

Famous Natives: William Faulkner (author), Jim Henson (puppeteer), Elvis Presley (singer, actor), Tennessee Williams (playwright)

State Greats: Vicksburg National Military Park and Cemetery, Natchez Trace

Fun Facts:
- Second state to leave the Union at the start of the Civil War (1861)
- Home to the first Coca-Cola® bottling plant
- Ancestral home of two Native American nations—the Chickasaw and the Natchez
- Home of the International Checkers Hall of Fame (Petal)

20th state

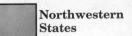
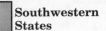

Missouri

Capital: Jefferson City
Population: 5,309,000
Size: 69,697 sq. miles

Statehood: August 10, 1821
State Bird: Bluebird
State Flower: Hawthorn
Nickname: The Show Me State
State Postal Abbreviation: MO

Famous Natives: Harry S. Truman (U.S. president), Martha Jane Canary, "Calamity Jane" (frontierswoman), Edwin Hubble (astronomer), Samuel Clemens, "Mark Twain" (author)

State Greats: Gateway Arch, Bagnell Dam

Fun Facts:
- Starting point for the Pony Express
- Starting point for the Lewis and Clark expedition (1804)
- State capital named for Thomas Jefferson, the 3rd president of the U.S.
- First slave state to free slaves (1865)

24th state

Montana

Capital: Helena
Population: 863,000
Size: 147,046 sq. miles

Statehood: November 8, 1889
State Bird: Western Meadowlark
State Flower: Bitterroot
Nickname: The Treasure State
State Postal Abbreviation: MT

Famous Natives: Lester Carl Thurow (economist), Harold Clayton Urey (chemist), Jeannette Rankin (first woman elected to U.S. Congress), Will James (author, artist)

State Greats: Little Big Horn, Glacier National Park, Giant Springs

Fun Facts:
- Home of Pompey's Pillar, a famous landmark used by early pioneers
- Custer's Last Stand took place south of Billings in 1876
- State name Montana comes for a Spanish word meaning mountain
- Largest grizzly bear population in the 48 contiguous states

41st state

Nebraska

Capital: Lincoln
Population: 1,649,000
Size: 77,355 sq. miles

Statehood: March 1, 1867
State Bird: Western Meadowlark
State Flower: Goldenrod
Nickname: The Cornhusker State
State Postal Abbreviation: NE

Famous Natives: Fred Astaire (dancer, actor), Grace Abbott (social worker), Harold Edgerton (inventor), Red Cloud (Indian rights advocate, leader)

State Greats: Chimney Rock, Nebraska National Forest

Fun Facts:
- Greater percentage of farmland than any other state
- Frozen dinners invented here
- More miles of river than any other state in the U.S.
- 911 system first developed and operated in Lincoln

37th state

Nevada

Capital: Carson City
Population: 1,206,000
Size: 110,561 sq. miles

Statehood: October 31, 1864
State Bird: Mountain Bluebird
State Flower: Sagebrush
Nickname: The Silver State
State Postal Abbreviation: NV

Famous Natives: Andre Agassi (tennis player), Sarah Winnemucca Hopkins (author, Paiute interpreter, peacemaker), Thelma Pat Nixon (U.S. presidential first lady), Waddie Mitchell (cowboy, author, recording artist)

State Greats: Hoover Dam, Lake Mead, Lake Tahoe

Fun Facts:
- Driest state
- More mountain ranges than any other state in the U.S.
- Largest gold producing state in the U.S.
- Native Indian tribes include Shoshone, Washo, and Paiute

36th state

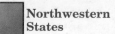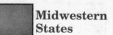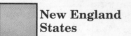
New Hampshire

Capital: Concord
Population: 1,114,000
Size: 9,279 sq. miles

Statehood: June 21, 1788
State Bird: Purple Finch
State Flower: Purple Lilac
Nickname: The Granite State
State Postal Abbreviation: NH

Famous Natives: Daniel Webster (statesman), Alan Shepard, Jr. (astronaut), Franklin Pierce (U.S. president), Augustus Saint-Gaudens (sculptor)

State Greats: Mt. Washington has fastest winds ever recorded (231 mph), "The Old Man of the Mountain"—a cliff side shaped like a human face

Fun Facts:
- State motto, "Live Free or Die"
- State where the first primary presidential election is held
- First state to declare independence from England
- Home of the first free public library, established in Peterborough, 1833

9th state

New Jersey

Capital: Trenton
Population: 7,878,000
Size: 7,787 sq. miles

Statehood: December 18, 1787
State Bird: Eastern Goldfinch
State Flower: Purple Violet
Nickname: The Garden State
State Postal Abbreviation: NJ

Famous Natives: Judy Blume (author), Aaron Burr (political leader), Walt Whitman (poet), Norman Schwarzkopf (army general)

State Greats: Princeton University, Thomas Edison's Menlo Park Laboratory

Fun Facts:
- First drive-in movie theater in the U.S. opened for business (1933)
- Telegraph invented (1844)
- Highest population density in the U.S.
- Home of Atlantic City, site of the world's largest boardwalk

3rd state

New Mexico

Capital: Santa Fe
Population: 1,685,000
Size: 121,593 sq. miles

Statehood: January 6, 1912
State Bird: Roadrunner
State Flower: Yucca Flower
Nickname: The Land of Enchantment
State Postal Abbreviation: NM

Famous Natives: Georgia O'Keefe (artist), William Hanna (animator), William "Buffalo Bill" Cody, (scout, showman), Dionisio Chavez (politician)

State Greats: Los Alamos/White Sands, Carlsbad Caverns, International UFO Museum and Research Center

Fun Facts:
- Location of El Camino Real, the oldest road built in the U.S. by Europeans
- Explored by the Spanish explorer Coronado (1540–1542)
- World's first atomic bomb was exploded (1945)
- Site of the world's largest annual hot air balloon festival, held in Albuquerque

47th state

New York

Capital: Albany
Population: 18,044,000
Size: 49,108 sq. miles

Statehood: July 26, 1788
State Bird: Bluebird
State Flower: Rose
Nickname: The Empire State
State Postal Abbreviation: NY

Famous Natives: George Eastman (inventor), Henry Louis Gehrig (baseball player), Franklin D. Roosevelt (U.S. president), Norman Rockwell (painter, illustrator)

State Greats: Ellis Island, Niagara Falls, New York City

Fun Facts:
- Home of the Baseball Hall of Fame (Cooperstown)
- Location of West Point Military Academy
- Home to Lake Placid, site of the Winter Olympic Games in 1932 and 1980
- Site of the first American chess tournament, held in 1843

11th state

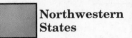 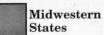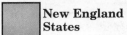
North Carolina — 12th state

Capital: Raleigh
Population: 6,658,000
Size: 52,699 sq. miles

Statehood: November 21, 1789
State Bird: Cardinal
State Flower: Dogwood
Nickname: The Tar Heel State
State Postal Abbreviation: NC

Famous Natives: Andrew Johnson (U.S. president), Dolley Madison (U.S. presidential first lady), Michael Jordan (basketball player), James K. Polk (U.S. president)

State Greats: Roanoke Island, Carl Sandburg's home, 66 American Revolution battle sites

Fun Facts:
• Location of Cape Hatteras, sometimes known as the "Graveyard of the Atlantic"
• Wright Brothers flew the world's first airplane at Kitty Hawk (1903)
• Location of Ocracoke Island, where Blackbeard the pirate had a hideout
• Leader in furniture and textile production in the U.S.

North Dakota — 39th state

Capital: Bismarck
Population: 641,000
Size: 70,702 sq. miles

Statehood: November 2, 1889
State Bird: Western Meadowlark
State Flower: Wild Prairie Rose
Nickname: The Peace Garden State
State Postal Abbreviation: ND

Famous Natives: Sitting Bull (Hunkpapa Sioux Indian chief), Lawrence Welk (band leader), Louis L'Amour (author)

State Greats: Theodore Roosevelt National Memorial Park

Fun Facts:
• Named after a Sioux word meaning "friends or allies"
• Leader in the production of barley and wheat in the U.S.
• Ranks first in the U.S. in total coal reserves
• Grows more sunflowers than any other state in the U.S.

Ohio — 17th state

Capital: Columbus
Population: 10,887,000
Size: 41,330 sq. miles

Statehood: March 1, 1803
State Bird: Cardinal
State Flower: Scarlet Carnation
Nickname: The Buckeye State
State Postal Abbreviation: OH

Famous Natives: John Glenn (astronaut, senator), Ulysses S. Grant (U.S. president), Neil Armstrong (astronaut), George Armstrong Custer (army officer)

State Greats: Rock and Roll Hall of Fame and Museum, Pro Football Hall of Fame

Fun Facts:
• Named after an Iroquois word meaning "beautiful"
• Birthplace of seven presidents
• Home to the first pro baseball team, the Cincinnati Red Stockings
• World's largest basket can be found in Basketville USA in Dresden

Oklahoma — 46th state

Capital: Oklahoma City
Population: 3,158,000
Size: 69,919 sq. miles

Statehood: November 16, 1907
State Bird: Scissor-tailed Flycatcher
State Flower: Mistletoe
Nickname: The Sooner State
State Postal Abbreviation: OK

Famous Natives: Will Rogers (humorist), Mickey Mantle (baseball player), Oral Roberts (evangelist), Maria Tallchief (ballerina)

State Greats: Cherokee Heritage Center, Will Rogers Memorial, National Cowboy Hall of Fame

Fun Facts:
• Working oil wells on the grounds of the state capitol building
• Location of the Chisholm Trail, along which cowboys drove cattle from Texas to Kansas
• More man-made lakes than any other state in the U.S.
• Largest Native American population than any state in the U.S.

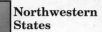
Oregon

Capital: Salem
Population: 2,854,000
Size: 97,073 sq. miles

Statehood: February 14, 1859
State Bird: Western Meadowlark
State Flower: Oregon Grape
Nickname: The Beaver State
State Postal Abbreviation: OR

Famous Natives: Raymond Carver (writer, poet), Beverly Cleary (author), Douglas Engelbart (inventor), Linus Carl Pauling (chemist)

State Greats: Crater Lake, Columbia River Gorge

Fun Facts:
• Bordered on the north by the Columbia River
• Location of the largest forest of lava-cast trees in the world
• Home of Crater Lake, the deepest lake in the U.S.
• Home of Carousel Museum, the world's largest collection of carousel horses

33rd state

Pennsylvania

Capital: Harrisburg
Population: 12,000,000
Size: 45,308 sq. miles

Statehood: December 12, 1787
State Bird: Ruffed Grouse
State Flower: Mountain Laurel
Nickname: The Keystone State
State Postal Abbreviation: PA

Famous Natives: James Buchanan (U.S. president), Louisa May Alcott (author), Margaret Mead (anthropologist), Betsy Ross (flagmaker)

State Greats: World's largest chocolate factory (Hershey), Liberty Bell

Fun Facts:
• Declaration of Independence signed in Philadelphia (1776)
• First baseball stadium built in the U.S. (Pittsburgh, 1909)
• Site of the first public zoo in the U.S., the Philadelphia Zoo
• Home of Punxsutawney Phil, the famous weather forecasting groundhog

2nd state

Rhode Island

Capital: Providence
Population: 1,006,000
Size: 1,212 sq. miles

Statehood: May 29, 1790
State Bird: Rhode Island Red
State Flower: Violet
Nickname: The Ocean State
State Postal Abbreviation: RI

Famous Natives: Oliver Hazard Perry (naval officer), Gilbert Stuart (painter), George M. Cohan (song writer), Robert Gray (sea captain)

State Greats: First Baptist church in the U.S.

Fun Facts:
• Smallest state in the U.S.
• Site of the oldest schoolhouse in the U.S. (Portsmouth, 1716)
• First colony to declare its independence from Britain (May 4, 1776)
• Ranks first in the U.S. in the production of costume jewelry
• Home of the Tennis Hall of Fame

13th state

South Carolina

Capital: Columbia
Population: 3,506,000
Size: 31,113 sq. miles

Statehood: May 23, 1788
State Bird: Carolina Wren
State Flower: Yellow Jessamine
Nickname: The Palmetto State
State Postal Abbreviation: SC

Famous Natives: Jesse Jackson (civil rights leader), David Robert Coker (inventor), Althea Gibson (tennis player), Ronald McNair (astronaut)

State Greats: Myrtle Beach, Hilton Head, Fort Sumter

Fun Facts:
• First shots of the Civil War fired in Fort Sumter
• First state to secede from the Union
• Home of the Grand Strand – a 60-mile stretch of beach that is also one of the most popular tourist attractions in the U.S.

8th state

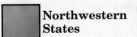

South Dakota

Capital: Pierre
Population: 732,000
Size: 77,116 sq. miles

Statehood: November 2, 1889
State Bird: Ring-Necked Pheasant
State Flower: American Pasque Flower
Nickname: The Mount Rushmore State
State Postal Abbreviation: SD

Famous Natives: Sitting Bull (Hunkpappa Sioux chief), Tom Brokaw (TV news anchor, writer), Sparky Anderson (baseball manager), Crazy Horse (Oglala Indian chief)

State Greats: Mount Rushmore, Badlands National Park, Crazy Horse Monument, Black Hills

Fun Facts:
- Location of the oldest continuously operating underground gold mine in the world
- Roughly divided in half by the Missouri River
- Home of the Dakota, Lakota, and Nakota Indian tribes that make up the Sioux nation
- U.S.S. Dakota – most decorated battleship in World War II

40th state

Tennessee

Capital: Nashville
Population: 4,897,000
Size: 42,144 sq. miles

Statehood: June 1, 1796
State Bird: Mockingbird
State Flower: Iris
Nickname: The Volunteer State
State Postal Abbreviation: TN

Famous Natives: Davy Crockett (frontiersman), Sequoia (Cherokee scholar), Hattie Caraway (first elected woman U.S. senator), Sam Davis (Confederate scout)

State Greats: National Civil Rights Museum, Grand Ole Opry, Great Smoky Mountains

Fun Facts:
- Bordered by eight states
- Location of Graceland, where Elvis Presley lived
- Birthplace of three presidents—Andrew Jackson, James K. Polk, and Andrew Johnson
- Home of the only monument in the U.S. honoring both Union and Confederate armies (Greeneville)

16th state

Texas

Capital: Austin
Population: 17,060,000
Size: 266,807 sq. miles

Statehood: December 29, 1845
State Bird: Mockingbird
State Flower: Bluebonnet
Nickname: The Lone Star State
State Postal Abbreviation: TX

Famous Natives: Dwight D. Eisenhower (general, U.S. president), Lyndon B. Johnson (U.S. president), Sandra Day O'Connor (1st woman U.S. Supreme Court justice), Sam Houston (general, statesman)

State Greats: The Alamo, Lyndon Johnson Space Center, Rio Grande River

Fun Facts:
- Second largest state in the U.S.
- Largest producer of wool in the U.S.
- More land farmed than any other state in the U.S.
- More species of bats live here than in any other part of the U.S.

28th state

Utah

Capital: Salt Lake City
Population: 1,728,000
Size: 84,899 sq. miles

Statehood: January 4, 1896
State Bird: Sea Gull
State Flower: Sego Lily
Nickname: The Beehive State
State Postal Abbreviation: UT

Famous Natives: Butch Cassidy (outlaw), Donny and Marie Osmond (singers, entertainers), Brigham Young (territory governor, religious leader), Philo T. Farnsworth (inventor)

State Greats: Bonneville Salt Flats, Great Salt Lake

Fun Facts:
- Site of the first transcontinental railway system in the U.S. (1869)
- Settled by Mormon leader Brigham Young and his followers
- Site of the nation's first department store
- Home of five national parks and seven national monuments

45th state

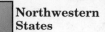 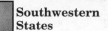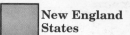
Vermont

Capital: Montpelier
Population: 565,000
Size: 9,614 sq. miles

Statehood: March 4, 1791
State Bird: Hermit Thrush
State Flower: Red Clover
Nickname: The Green Mountain State
State Postal Abbreviation: VT

Famous Natives: Chester A. Arthur (U.S. president), Calvin Coolidge (U.S. president), John Deere (inventor), George Dewey (admiral)

State Greats: Largest granite quarries in U.S.

Fun Facts:
- Only New England state without a seacoast
- Explored by Samuel de Champlain (1609)
- Leading producer of maple syrup in the U.S.
- First state to abolish slavery (1791)

14th state

Virginia

Capital: Richmond
Population: 6,217,000
Size: 40,767 sq. miles

Statehood: June 25, 1788
State Bird: Cardinal
State Flower: Dogwood
Nickname: The Old Dominion
State Postal Abbreviation: VA

Famous Natives: Patrick Henry (statesman), Edgar Allan Poe (author), Robert E. Lee (Confederate general), Arthur Ashe (tennis player)

State Greats: Mount Vernon, Jamestown settlement

Fun Facts:
- Birthplace of eight presidents
- Both the American Revolution and the Civil War ended in this state
- Over half of the battles fought in the Civil War were fought in this state
- Home of the world's largest office building, the Pentagon in Arlington

10th state

Washington

Capital: Olympia
Population: 4,888,000
Size: 68,139 sq. miles

Statehood: November 11, 1889
State Bird: Willow Goldfinch
State Flower: Coast Rhododendron
Nickname: The Evergreen State
State Postal Abbreviation: WA

Famous Natives: Bill Gates (software executive), Douglas D. Anderson (archaeologist), Bob Barker (TV host), John W. Kendall (scientist)

State Greats: Olympic National Park, Grand Coulee Dam, Mount Ranier

Fun Facts:
- Site of Mount Saint Helens, the volcano that erupted in 1980
- Home of the Space Needle, a tower over 600 feet tall
- Only state to be named for a U.S. president
- Produces more apples than any other state in the U.S.

42nd state

West Virginia

Capital: Charleston
Population: 1,802,000
Size: 24,232 sq. miles

Statehood: June 20, 1863
State Bird: Cardinal
State Flower: Rhododendron
Nickname: The Mountain State
State Postal Abbreviation: WV

Famous Natives: Pearl S. Buck (author), Mary Lou Retton (gymnast), John Brown (abolitionist), Chuck Yeager (test pilot and Air Force general)

State Greats: Smoke Hole Caverns, National Radio Astronomy Observatory, White Sulphur Springs

Fun Facts:
- Completely covered by the Appalachian Mountains
- Location of Harper's Ferry, where John Brown made his famous raid
- Part of Virginia until the Civil War—West Virginians chose to stay in the Union
- Site of the first 4-H camp in the U.S. (Jackson's Mill)

35th state

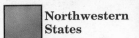
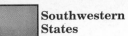

Wisconsin

Capital: Madison
Population: 4,907,000
Size: 56,153 sq. miles

Statehood: May 29, 1848
State Bird: Robin
State Flower: Wood Violet
Nickname: The Badger State
State Postal Abbreviation: WI

Famous Natives: Harry Houdini (magician), Charles and John Ringling (circus entrepreneurs), Georgia O'Keefe (painter), Laura Ingalls Wilder (author)

State Greats: Circus World Museum, Nicolet National Forest

Fun Facts:
- Explored by Jean Nicolet (1634)
- Named for an Ojibway word meaning "gathering of the waters"
- Home of the first kindergarten in the U.S. (Watertown, 1856)
- Leader in milk and cheese production in the U.S.

30th state

Wyoming

Capital: Cheyenne
Population: 456,000
Size: 97,809 sq. miles

Statehood: July 10, 1890
State Bird: Western Meadowlark
State Flower: Indian Paintbrush
Nickname: The Equality State
State Postal Abbreviation: WY

Famous Natives: John Colter (trader), John Phillips (frontiersman), Francis W. Warren (first state governor), Chief Nashakie (Shoshone chief)

State Greats: Old Faithful, Yellowstone National Park

Fun Facts:
- Also known as the "Cowboy State"
- First state to grant women the right to vote (1869)
- Least populated of all states
- Home of Devils Tower, the first national monument designated in the U.S. (1906)

44th state

Washington, D.C.

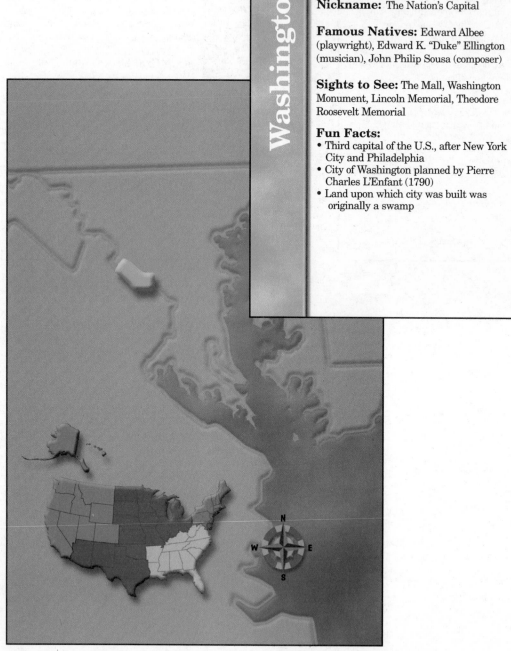

Became U.S. Capital:
December 1, 1800
Population: 585,000
Size: 67 sq. miles

Official Bird: Wood Thrush
Official Flower: American Beauty Rose
Nickname: The Nation's Capital

Famous Natives: Edward Albee
(playwright), Edward K. "Duke" Ellington
(musician), John Philip Sousa (composer)

Sights to See: The Mall, Washington
Monument, Lincoln Memorial, Theodore
Roosevelt Memorial

Fun Facts:
- Third capital of the U.S., after New York
  City and Philadelphia
- City of Washington planned by Pierre
  Charles L'Enfant (1790)
- Land upon which city was built was
  originally a swamp

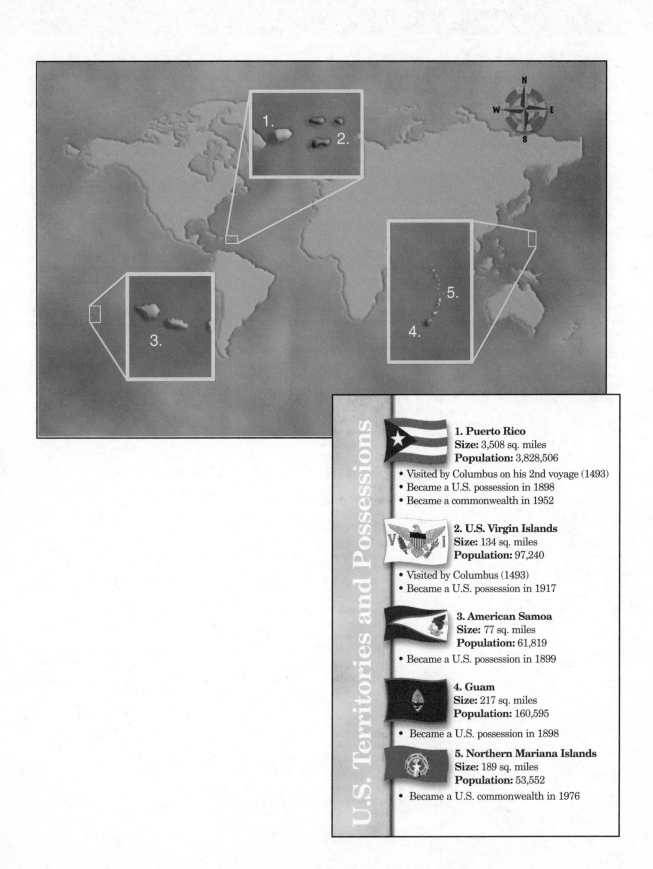

U.S. Territories and Possessions

1. Puerto Rico
Size: 3,508 sq. miles
Population: 3,828,506

- Visited by Columbus on his 2nd voyage (1493)
- Became a U.S. possession in 1898
- Became a commonwealth in 1952

2. U.S. Virgin Islands
Size: 134 sq. miles
Population: 97,240

- Visited by Columbus (1493)
- Became a U.S. possession in 1917

3. American Samoa
Size: 77 sq. miles
Population: 61,819

- Became a U.S. possession in 1899

4. Guam
Size: 217 sq. miles
Population: 160,595

- Became a U.S. possession in 1898

5. Northern Mariana Islands
Size: 189 sq. miles
Population: 53,552

- Became a U.S. commonwealth in 1976

U.S. Historical Facts

1492 - Christopher Columbus discovers New World.

1497 - John Cabot makes first voyage to North America for England.

1499 - Florentine merchant Amerigo Vespucci visits New World.

1507 - German mapmaker Martin Waldseemüller names New World *America* after Amerigo Vespucci.

1513 - Juan Ponce de León discovers Florida.

1540 - Francisco Vásques de Coronado discovers the Grand Canyon while exploring the Southwest.

1541 - Francisco Vásques de Coronado discovers the Mississippi River.

1565 - Spaniards establish St. Augustine, Florida, the first permanent European settlement in the United States.

1585 - Sir Walter Raleigh establishes England's first American colony at Roanoke Island, off the coast of North Carolina.

1590 - Colony at Roanoke Island disappears.

1607 - Approximately 100 colonists establish Jamestown, Virginia, the first permanent British settlement in America.

1619 - Virginia establishes the *House of Burgesses*, the first representative legislature in America.

1620 - Pilgrims establish *Plymouth Colony* at Plymouth, Massachusetts — the second permanent British settlement in America — and draw up *Mayflower Compact*.

1636 - Harvard — the first college in the colonies — is established.

1647 - Massachusetts establishes the first colonial public school system.

1649 - Maryland passes the first religious toleration act in North America.

1652 - Rhode Island becomes the first colony to outlaw slavery; the first American coins are minted in Boston.

1661 - Virginia becomes the first colony to recognize slavery as being legal.

1690 - Massachusetts issues the first colonial paper money.

1704 - *The Boston News-Letter* — the first successful colonial newspaper — begins publication.

1752 - Benjamin Franklin flies a homemade kite during a storm, proving that lightning is a form of electricity.

1754 - *French and Indian War* begins.

1763 - *French and Indian War* ends with the *Treaty of Paris*.

1765 - British Parliament passes *Stamp Act*, taxing newspapers, legal documents, and other printed materials in the colonies.

1770 - British troops kill five American civilians in the *Boston Massacre*.

1773 - *Boston Tea Party* is staged when colonists dump British tea into Boston Harbor.

1774 - *Intolerable Acts* close Boston Harbor to punish colonists for *Boston Tea Party*; *First Continental Congress* meets in Philadelphia, Pennsylvania.

1775 - *Revolutionary War* begins; *Second Continental Congress* meets in Philadelphia, Pennsylvania.

1776 - *Declaration of Independence* is adopted; the United States of America is formed.

1777 - *Articles of Confederation* are endorsed; Stars and Stripes flag is adopted; Washington's army winters at Valley Forge, Pennsylvania.

1780 - Pennsylvania becomes first state to abolish slavery.

1781 - Last major battle of the *Revolutionary War* is fought between America and Britain in Yorktown, Virginia; *Articles of Confederation* take effect.

1783 - *Revolutionary War* ends with the *Treaty of Paris*.

1787 - *Constitution* is written by Founding Fathers.

1789 - George Washington elected as first president.

1791 - *Bill of Rights* comes into effect; First Bank of the United States opens.

1792 - Construction of the White House begins.

1793 - Congress passes a fugitive slave law requiring the return of runaway slaves.

1798 - Georgia becomes the last state to abolish slavery.

1800 - Washington, D.C. becomes the national capital.

1803 - *Louisiana Purchase* nearly doubles the size of the United States.

1804 - Lewis and Clark expedition departs from St. Louis, Missouri.

1808 - African slave trade ends.

1812 - *War of 1812* begins.

1814 - Francis Scott Key writes "The Star-Spangled Banner"; *War of 1812* ends with *Treaty of Ghent*.

1823 - *Monroe Doctrine* warns Europeans against interfering in Western Hemisphere affairs.

1835 - Samuel F. B. Morse invents the telegraph; Erie Canal opens.

1846 - *Mexican War* begins.

1848 - *Mexican War* ends with *Treaty of Guadalupe-Hidalgo*; discovery of gold in California triggers the *Gold Rush*.

1856 - America's first kindergarten opens in Watertown, Wisconsin.

1858 - *Lincoln-Douglas Debates* focus on slavery.

1860 - *Pony Express* is established.

1861 - *Civil War* begins at Fort Sumter; *Pony Express* ends.

1863 - *Emancipation Proclamation* declares all slaves freed from Confederate-held territory.

1865 - *Civil War* ends with Lee's surrender to Grant at Appomattox, Virginia; *13th Amendment* outlaws slavery throughout the United States.

1867 - United States buys Alaska from Russia for $7.2 million.

1868 - *14th Amendment* grants equality.

1870 - *15th Amendment* guarantees most male citizens the right to vote.

1876 - Alexander Graham Bell invents the telephone.

1877 - Thomas Edison invents the phonograph.

1879 - Thomas Edison invents the electric light bulb.

1898 - *Spanish-American War* is fought.

1906 - Theodore Roosevelt becomes first American to win *Nobel Peace Prize*.

1913 - *16th Amendment* allows the federal government to collect income tax.

1914 - *World War I* begins.

1917 - United States enters *World War I*.

1918 - *Armistice Day* ends *World War I*.

1929 - Stock Market crashes; *Great Depression* begins.

1939 - *World War II* begins.

1941 - Bombing of Pearl Harbor on Dec. 7 prompts United States to enter *World War II*.

1945 - Japan surrenders — ending *World War II* — after bombs are dropped on Hiroshima and Nagasaki.

1950 - *Korean War* begins.

1953 - *Korean War* ends with armistice.

1957 - *Vietnam War* begins.

1962 - *Cuban Missile Crisis* takes place.

1964 - *Civil Rights Act of 1964* allows all people to be served in restaurants, hotels, and businesses.

1969 - On July 20, Neil Armstrong and Buzz Aldrin of Apollo XI become first men to walk on the moon.

1972 - Congress passes *Equal Rights Amendment*.

1975 - *Vietnam War* ends with the surrender of South Vietnam to North Vietnam.

1991 - *Persian Gulf War* or "Operation Desert Storm" begins (ends in 1992).

2000 - As the new millennium begins, fears of the "Y2K bug" pass without problems around the world.

2001 - On September 11, terrorists hijack 4 planes and crash them into New York, Washington D.C., and Pennsylvania, causing the worst act of terrorism against America in U.S. history.

2001 - War on Terrorism begins in response to the September 11th attacks. Countries around the world join together to fight terrorism.

U.S. Presidents

No.	President	Term	Born	Died	Vice-President
1ST	George Washington	Apr. 30, 1789 - Mar. 3, 1797	Feb. 22, 1732	Dec. 14, 1799	John Adams (1789-1797)
2ND	John Adams (F)	Mar. 4, 1797 - Mar. 3, 1801	Oct. 30, 1735	July 4, 1826	Thomas Jefferson (1797-1801)
3RD	Thomas Jefferson (DR)	Mar. 4, 1801 - Mar. 3, 1809	Apr. 13, 1743	July 4, 1826	Aaron Burr (1801-1805) George Clinton (1805-1809)
4TH	James Madison (DR)	Mar. 4, 1809 - Mar. 3, 1817	Mar. 16, 1751	June 28, 1836	George Clinton (1809-1812) Elbridge Gerry (1813-1814)
5TH	James Monroe (DR)	Mar. 4, 1817 - Mar. 3, 1825	Apr. 28, 1758	July 4, 1831	Daniel D. Tompkins (1817-1825)
6TH	John Quincy Adams (DR)	Mar. 4, 1825 - Mar. 3, 1829	July 11, 1767	Feb. 23, 1848	John C. Calhoun (1825-1829)
7TH	Andrew Jackson (D)	Mar. 4, 1829 - Mar. 3, 1837	Mar. 15, 1767	June 8, 1845	John C. Calhoun (1829-1832) Martin Van Buren (1833-1837)
8TH	Martin Van Buren (D)	Mar. 4, 1837 - Mar. 3, 1841	Dec. 5, 1782	July 24, 1862	Richard M. Johnson (1837-1841)
9TH	William H. Harrison (W)	Mar. 4, 1841 - Apr. 4, 1841	Feb. 9, 1773	Apr. 4, 1841	John Tyler (1841)
10TH	John Tyler (W/SD)	Apr. 6, 1841 - Mar. 3, 1845	Mar. 29, 1790	Jan. 18, 1862	
11TH	James K. Polk (D)	Mar. 4, 1845 - Mar. 3, 1849	Nov. 2, 1795	June 15, 1849	George M. Dallas (1845-1849)
12TH	Zachary Taylor (W)	Mar. 4, 1849 - July 9, 1850	Nov. 24, 1784	July 9, 1850	Millard Fillmore (1849-1850)
13TH	Millard Fillmore (W)	July 10, 1850 - Mar. 3, 1853	Jan. 7, 1800	Mar. 8, 1874	
14TH	Franklin Pierce (D)	Mar. 4, 1853 - Mar. 3, 1857	Nov. 23, 1804	Oct. 8, 1869	William R. King (1853)
15TH	James Buchanan (D)	Mar. 4, 1857 - Mar. 3, 1861	Apr. 23, 1791	June 1, 1868	John C. Breckinridge (1857-1861)
16TH	Abraham Lincoln (R)	Mar. 4, 1861 - Apr. 15, 1865	Feb. 12, 1809	Apr. 15, 1865	Hannibal Hamlin (1861-1865) Andrew Johnson (1865)
17TH	Andrew Johnson (D/U)	Apr. 15, 1865 - Mar. 3, 1869	Dec. 29, 1808	July 31, 1875	
18TH	Ulysses S. Grant (R)	Mar. 4, 1869 - Mar. 3, 1877	Apr. 27, 1822	July 23, 1885	Schuyler Colfax (1869-1873) Henry Wilson (1873-1875)
19TH	Rutherford B. Hayes (R)	Mar. 4, 1877 - Mar. 3, 1881	Oct. 4, 1822	Jan. 17, 1893	William A. Wheeler (1877-1881)
20TH	James A. Garfield (R)	Mar. 4, 1881 - Sept. 19, 1881	Nov. 19, 1831	Sept. 19, 1881	Chester A. Arthur (1881)
21ST	Chester A. Arthur (R)	Sept. 20, 1881 - Mar. 3, 1885	Oct. 5, 1829	Nov. 18, 1886	
22ND	Grover Cleveland (D)	Mar. 4, 1885 - Mar. 3, 1889	Mar. 18, 1837	June 24, 1908	Thomas A. Hendricks (1885)
23RD	Benjamin Harrison (R)	Mar. 4, 1889 - Mar. 3, 1893	Aug. 20, 1833	Mar. 13, 1901	Levi P. Morton (1889-1893)
24TH	Grover Cleveland (D)	Mar. 4, 1893 - Mar. 3, 1897	Mar. 18, 1837	June 24, 1908	Adlai E. Stevenson (1893-1897)
25TH	William McKinley (R)	Mar. 4, 1897 - Sept. 14, 1901	Jan. 29, 1843	Sept. 14, 1901	Garret A. Hobart (1897-1899) Theodore Roosevelt (1901)
26TH	Theodore Roosevelt (R)	Sept. 14, 1901 - Mar. 3, 1909	Oct. 27, 1858	Jan. 6, 1919	Charles W. Fairbanks (1905-1909)
27TH	William H. Taft (R)	Mar. 4, 1909 - Mar. 3, 1913	Sept. 15, 1857	Mar. 8, 1930	James S. Sherman (1909-1912)
28TH	Woodrow Wilson (D)	Mar. 4, 1913 - Mar. 3, 1921	Dec. 29, 1856	Feb. 3, 1924	Thomas R. Marshall (1913-1921)
29TH	Warren G. Harding (R)	Mar. 4, 1921 - Aug. 2, 1923	Nov. 2, 1865	Aug. 2, 1923	Calvin Coolidge (1921-1923)
30TH	Calvin Coolidge (R)	Aug. 3, 1923 - Mar. 3, 1929	July 4, 1872	Jan. 5, 1933	Charles G. Dawes (1925-1929)
31ST	Herbert C. Hoover (R)	Mar. 4, 1929 - Mar. 3, 1933	Aug. 10, 1874	Oct. 20, 1964	Charles Curtis (1929-1933)
32ND	Franklin D. Roosevelt (D)	Mar. 4, 1933 - Apr. 12, 1945	Jan. 30, 1882	Apr. 12, 1945	John N. Garner (1933-1941) Henry A. Wallace (1941-1945) Harry S. Truman (1945)
33RD	Harry S. Truman (D)	Apr. 12, 1945 - Jan. 20, 1953	May 8, 1884	Dec. 26, 1972	Alben W. Barkley (1949-1953)
34TH	Dwight D. Eisenhower(R)	Jan. 20, 1953 - Jan. 20, 1961	Oct. 14, 1890	Mar. 28, 1969	Richard M. Nixon (1953-1961)
35TH	John F. Kennedy (D)	Jan. 20, 1961 - Nov. 22, 1963	May 29, 1917	Nov. 22, 1963	Lyndon B. Johnson (1961-1963)
36TH	Lyndon B. Johnson (D)	Nov. 22, 1963 - Jan. 20, 1969	Aug. 27, 1908	Jan. 22, 1973	Hubert H. Humphrey (1965-1969)
37TH	Richard M. Nixon (R)	Jan. 20, 1969 - Aug. 9, 1974	Jan. 9, 1913	Apr. 22, 1994	Spiro T. Agnew (1969-1973) Gerald R. Ford (1973-1974)[1]
38TH	Gerald R. Ford (R)[2]	Aug. 9, 1974 - Jan. 20, 1977	July 14, 1913		Nelson A. Rockefeller (1974-1977)[3]
39TH	Jimmy Carter (D)	Jan. 20, 1977 - Jan. 20, 1981	Oct. 1, 1924		Walter F. Mondale (1977-1981)
40TH	Ronald W. Reagan (R)	Jan. 20, 1981 - Jan. 20, 1989	Feb. 6, 1911	June 5, 2004	George H. W. Bush (1981-1989)
41ST	George H. W. Bush (R)	Jan. 20, 1989 - Jan. 20, 1993	June 12, 1924		Dan Quayle (1989-1993)
42ND	Bill Clinton (D)	Jan. 20, 1993 - Jan. 20, 2001	Aug. 19, 1946		Al Gore (1993-2001)
43RD	George W. Bush (R)	Jan. 20, 2001 -	July 6, 1946		Richard B. Cheney (2001-)

D = Democratic Party
DR = Democratic-Republican Party
F = Federalist Party
R = Republican Party

SD = Southern Democrat
U = Union or Republican & War Democrat
W = Whig Party

[1]Inaugurated December 6, 1973, replacing Agnew, who resigned October 10, 1973.
[2]Inaugurated August 9, 1974, replacing Nixon, who resigned that same day.
[3]Inaugurated December 19, 1974, replacing Ford, who became President August 9, 1974.

Regional Native American Tribes

Great Plains Native Americans	Iowa, Kansa, Missouri, Wichita, Comanche, Omaha, Crow, Cheyenne, Sioux, Lakota	
Spotlight on: Cheyenne Tribe		
Region	North American Plains near the Platte and Arkansas rivers; in the Black Hills of South Dakota; tall grasslands and rivers	
Climate	warm, dry summers; cold winters with blowing snow	
Shelter	tepees were made of long poles and buffalo skins which could be easily taken apart and moved	
Resources	buffalo used for fuel, food, and clothing; fertile river valley allowed for some farming	

Northeast Native Americans (Eastern Woodlands)	Mohawk, Cayuga, Seneca, Oneida, Onondaga, Iroquois, Delaware	
Spotlight on: Seneca Tribe		
Region	western New York and eastern Ohio	
Climate	warm summers; cold, snowy winters	
Shelter	longhouses built of wood and bark	
Resources	Fertile soil and an abundance of fresh water from the Great Lakes allowed them to cultivate corn and other vegetables; hunted a variety of wild game	

Northwest Native Americans	Makah, Haida, Okanagoh, Quinault, Nootka, Chinook, Spokane, Kalapuya, Kalispel, Shuswap

Spotlight on: Makah Tribe	
Region	Northwest Pacific coast of North America; Vancouver Island at northwest tip of Washington state
Climate	mild temperatures and heavy rainfall
Shelter	wooden plank houses
Resources	forests for shelter; salmon, whale, and caribou used for food

Southeast Native Americans	Cherokee, Chickasaw, Choctaw, Creek, Seminole, Powhatan, Natchez, Timicua, Sauk, Caddo

Spotlight on: Cherokee Tribe	
Region	Southern Appalachian region; North Carolina and Tennessee
Climate	mild seasons: warm summers and wet winters
Shelter	wigwams: huts with arched frameworks of poles covered with bark or animal hides
Resources	rich soil for farming crops of corn, beans, and squash, along with hunting wild game such as deer and birds

Southwest Native Americans	Navajo, Apache, Hopi, Pima, Pueblo, Papago, Cochimi

Spotlight on: Navajo Tribe	
Region	Four Corners—where Utah, Colorado, Arizona, and New Mexico meet; desert terrain with many cliffs, canyons, and rock formations
Climate	hot and dry with little rain
Shelter	hogans: houses built of logs and mud
Resources	desert soil good for growing crops such as beans, cotton, and corn; also used to make clay for pottery

Trails Across the Western Frontier

	Physical Features	Native Peoples	Food	Difficulties Along the Way
Oregon Trail	• rugged terrain of the Black Hills; Rocky Mountains; dry, sandy areas with rough, rocky ground; swift rivers and streams; trees and bunch grasses	• Sioux Native Americans • traded moccasins and beads for bread • sold salmon to pioneers • used buffalo dung for fuel	• wild game, including buffalo • mountain goats and lions • whales and otters	• scarlet fever, mumps, cholera, mosquito fever; rattlesnakes, disagreements with Native Americans
National Road	• Ohio, Scioto, Miami, and Wabash rivers; Appalachian Mountains; trees, wild onions, and mushrooms	• Shawnee and Miami Native Americans	• wild game, including deer • rabbits and wild turkeys	• steep slopes, narrow roads, and sharp turns of the Appalachian Mountains
Mormon Trail	• plains of Iowa and Nebraska; Platte River; Rocky Mountains; trees, grasses, wild flowers, and berries	• Arapaho, Omaha, and Iowa Native Americans	• wild game, including buffalo, deer, and elk	• scarlet fever, cholera, rattlesnakes, disagreements with Native Americans
California Trail	• Humboldt River; Nevada desert; Sierra Nevada Mountains in California; tumbleweeds, cactus, prairie grasses, and trees		• mountain goats, coyotes, and other wild game	• cholera and dysentery; snowstorms
Santa Fe Trail	• tall grasses over six feet high; Jornada del Muerto desert; Rocky Mountains; trees	• Comanche Native Americans • used buffalo dung for fuel	• buffalo, deer, antelope, and other wild game	• got lost in the tall grasses; harsh desert conditions

Sources: *The Story of America's Roads*, Ray Spangenburg and D. M. Moser 1992; *From Trail to Turnpikes*, Tim McNeese, 1993; *World Book Encyclopedia*, 1991.

 GLOSSARY

arid: dry

artificial boundaries: boundaries formed when people choose a place to draw a line

bay: part of a sea that is partly surrounded by land, smaller than a gulf

boundary: an imaginary line between two states or countries

butte: an isolated, flat-topped mountain, or hill

canal: an inland waterway built to carry water for the purpose of navigation or irrigation

canyon: a deep valley with steep sides, usually with a stream running through it

cape: a point of land that extends into the water

census: a counting, which happens every ten years, of the people living in the United States

cliff: a high, steep face of a rock

coast: land along the sea

coastal plain: the flat stretch of land along a shore

compass: shows which way north, south, east, and west are on a map

continental divide: an imaginary line running along the Rocky Mountains that divides the rivers that flow east from the ones that flow west

continents: one of the seven land areas of Earth, including Asia, North America, South America Africa, Antarctica, Europe, Australia

dam: a piece of land that holds back the flow of a body of water

degrees: a unit used to measure distance and location on Earth's surface

delta: an area of land formed by sediment at the mouth of a river

desert: a place where more water is lost due to evaporation than falls as precipitation

diversity: having many differences

dune: a mound, hill, or ridge of sand that is formed by wind

earthquake: a sudden shaking or shock inside Earth that causes movement on its surface

ecology: relationships between the living and nonliving things in an environment

ecosystem: a group of living organisms that depend on one another and the environment in which they live

elevation: altitude above sea level

elevation key: a part of a map that helps the reader understand the shape of the land

elevation/relief: the height of the land above sea level

equator: an imaginary line encircling Earth halfway between the North and South poles; degrees of latitude are measured from it

erosion: a process that strips rock and soil away from the surface of Earth and moves them to another place

evaporate: to change to water vapor

fall line: a line on rivers where waterfalls and rapids begin

fault: a break in Earth's crust along which rock masses have been moved with respect to one another

globe: a model of Earth that shows the correct shapes of Earth's major land masses and bodies of water

gorge: a deep, narrow opening between steep and rocky sides of walls or mountains

grid: a system of longitude and latitude; helps find places on the map

harbor: a deep body of water where ships can anchor

historical map: a physical or political map that shows borders, physical features, or events of the past

human region: an area that might be defined by the characteristics of its people, such as their language or government

Ice Age: any prehistoric period when ice sheets and glaciers covered much of Earth's surface; last Ice Age was 18,000 years ago

index: an alphabetical list of the places shown on the map

International Date Line: an imaginary line running approximately along the 180th meridian, marking the time boundary between one day and the next

immigrant: a person who settles in another country

irrigation systems: systems of channels, streams, or pipes used to bring water to crops

isthmus: a narrow strip of land bordered by water and connecting two larger bodies of land

labels: words/phrases that identify the symbols on a map

lagoon: a shallow area of ocean water partly or completely enclosed within an atoll; shallow body of seawater partly cut off from the sea by a narrow strip of land

large-scale map: a map that shows much detail

latitude lines: horizontal lines north and south of the equator

legend (or key): a list of the map's symbols and what they represent

lock: an enclosure, as in a canal, with gates at each end used in raising or lowering boats as they pass from one level to another

longitude lines (or meridians): vertical lines running from north to south on the globe

map: a flat drawing of Earth

map scale: shows how many miles/kilometers the inches/centimeters on a map represent

mesa: a large, flat-topped hill or mountain with steep sides surrounded by a plain

mouth: the place where a river empties into a larger body of water

natural boundaries: boundaries formed by physical features such as river

physical map: a map that shows physical features such as mountains, rivers, oceans, and deserts

plate tectonics: Earth's outer crust is made up of huge slabs of rock called plates; these plates move about below Earth's surface in ways called faulting and folding; this process is called plate tectonics

plateau: an area of relatively flat land elevated above the surrounding land

political map: a map that shows borders of states and countries and the location of capitals and other cities and towns

pollutants: something that pollutes, especially industrial waste or other material that contaminates the air, water, or soil

population density: the amount of people per unit of land area

port: a place with a harbor where ships can anchor

prime meridian: the starting point to measure both east and west around the globe; located in Greenwich, England

reef: a ridge of sand, rock, or coral that lies near the surface of a body of water

region: an area of Earth having one or more common characteristics; can be physical or human characteristics

relief map: a map that shows high points and low points of a land area

reservoir: a natural or human-made place used for the storage of water

savanna: a tropical grassland area

scale: shows the measurement of distances and areas

semi-desert: a dry area with very sparse vegetation, often located between a desert and a grassland

silt: a layer of fine mud

sound: a long, narrow body of water that runs parallel to the coast

sphere: an object shaped like a ball

strait: a narrow waterway or channel connecting two larger bodies of water

terrain: a region or tract of land, especially with regard to its natural features or suitability for some special purpose, such as farming

topography: physical features

toxic: of, relating to, or caused by poison

transcontinental railroad: a railroad that crosses a whole continent

tributary: a river or stream that flows into a larger river or stream

tsunami: waves in the ocean caused by earthquakes

urbanization: the movement to, and clustering of, people in cities

valley: the lower land that lies between hills and mountains

volcano: an opening in Earth's crust from which ashes and hot gases flow

waterfall: a flow of water from a high place over a ledge

watershed: area drained by a river system

wetlands: areas that have wet soils, such as swamps and marshes

NOTES

MAP SKILLS

You know that the United States is divided into several major regions. Some are physical regions, like the Rocky Mountains and the deserts of the Southwest; some are human regions such as the Corn Belt and the Dixie. Maps can show the borders and names of these regions.

A. Look at the below map of the United States and complete the following.

1. Locate your state on the map and write your state name below.

_____

2. If you were describing the general area of the United States in which your state is located, which one of the following would you choose? Check one.

        the South   the North   the East   the West

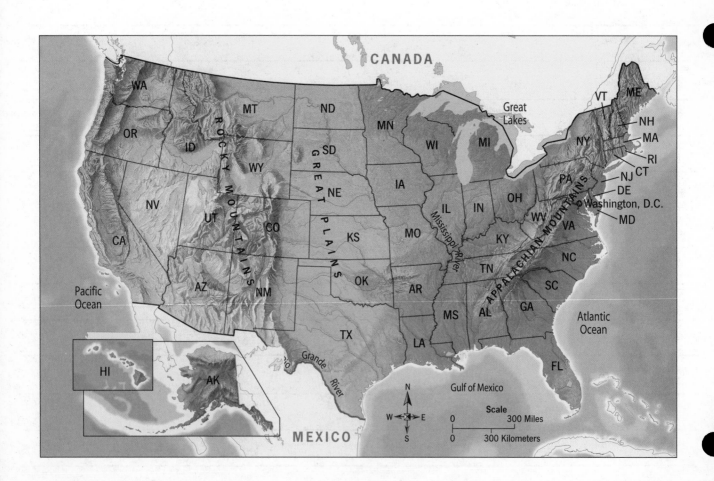

B. Think about where you live in the United States.

   1. Write the names of the states near your state that you think have similar features—such as beaches, mountains, forests, or weather—to your state.

   _____   _____

   _____   _____

   2. If you could give your state, together with the ones you listed above, a "region" name, what would you call the region? Think about features the states share and write a region name below.

   _____

C. Looking at the map, think about what you know about the different areas of our country. What makes each area special or unique? How would you divide the United States into regions?

   1. Write the names of the regions you would include.

     a. _____   **d.** _____

     b. _____   **e.** _____

     c. _____   **f.** _____

   2. Make notes about where you will draw the borders for each region.

   _____

   _____

   _____

   _____

D. Compare your map with the regional maps in the article.

   1. Does your map have the same number of regions? _____

   2. Which, if any, borders are alike, and which are different? Why do you think the same or different borders were chosen?

   _____

   _____

MAP SKILLS Using Physical and Thematic Maps

One of California's biggest problems has been earthquakes that occur along the San Andreas Fault. A fault is a fracture or break in Earth's crust. The San Andreas Fault is one of the most active in the world and is very dangerous. While most faults lie deep beneath Earth's surface, some, like the San Andreas Fault, are visible. It looks like a gash in the land.

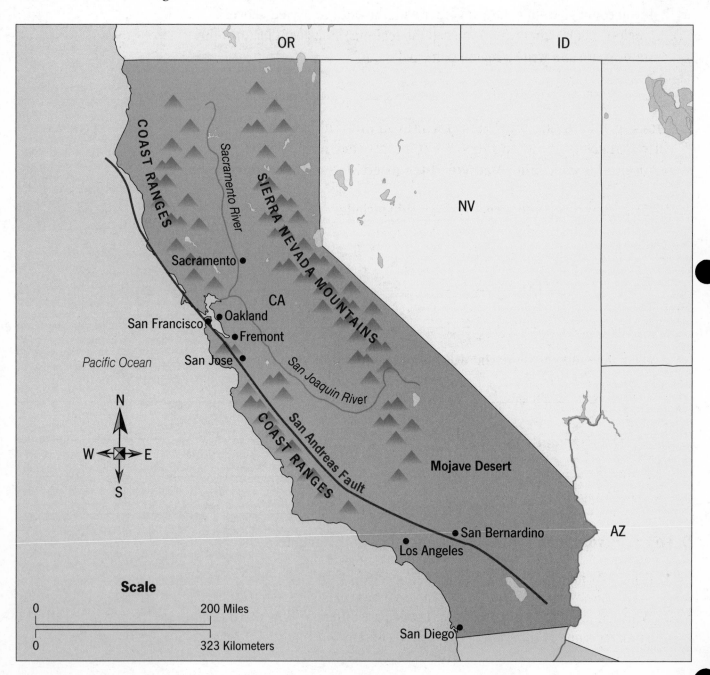

A. Study the physical map of California. Use the information on the map to complete the following.

1. Trace the line of the San Andreas Fault on the map.

2. How long is the San Andreas Fault? _____

3. What major cities are located on or near the fault? _____

_____

4. Write a brief description of where the fault is located, including where

it begins and ends. _____

_____

B. Continue to study the map, particularly the San Andreas Fault. Complete the following.

1. Which California city has been hit by two severe earthquakes, one

in 1906 and another in 1989? _____

_____

2. Use the chart below to describe the city, including where in California it is located and its land and water features.

City Name	
Where It Is Located	
Land and Water Features	

3. Do you think the city's location makes it more vulnerable to the activity of the San Andreas Fault than other cities located along the Fault? Why?

_____

_____

4. How does the San Andreas Fault affect life in California? _____

_____

69

Specific terms are used to identify Earth's landforms and water forms. The below diagram shows some of these terms.

butte – an isolated mountain or hill with a small flat top

cape – a narrow point of land that sticks out into the water

cliff – a steep face of rock or earth

delta – a fan-shaped piece of land formed by soil that drops from a river at its mouth

dune – a mound of loose sand that is shaped by blowing wind

lagoon – a shallow body of water that opens onto the sea

mesa – a mountain or hill with a large flat top

mouth – the place where a river empties into a larger body of water

reef – a narrow chain of coral, rock, and sand above or below the water

reservoir – a natural or artificially made place used to store water

sound – a long, wide body of water that separates an island from the mainland; parallel to the coast

strait – a narrow body of water that connects two larger bodies of water

tributary – a river or stream that flows into a larger river or stream

waterfall – a stream that flows over the edge of a cliff

A. Using the diagram, list the different forms of land and water in the appropriate columns below.

Landforms	Water Forms

B. Identify the landforms and water forms described below and complete the puzzle.

1. A stream that flows over the edge of a cliff. __ __ __ __ __ __ __ __ __

2. A narrow body of water that connects two larger bodies of water. __ __ __ __ __ __

3. A river or stream that flows into a larger river or stream. __ __ __ __ __ __ __ __ __ __

4. The place where a river empties into a larger body of water. __ __ __ __ __

5. A point of land that extends into the water. __ __ __ __

C. The following landforms and water forms are also on the map, but are not labeled. Label them.

1. mountain   **6.** volcano
2. river   **7.** glacier
3. ocean   **8.** bay
4. plateau   **9.** canal
5. hill   **10.** valley

D. Turn to the world map in the Almanac on pages 2-3. How many other forms of land and water can you find?

_____

_____

MAP SKILLS
Using a Map to Trace Expeditioners' Routes and Divide the Land

Maps can show the movement of people across an area of land. The map below uses colored arrows and different types of lines, for example, a solid versus a dotted line, to indicate different routes. The physical features of the routes are included on the map in order to show the geography encountered along the way.

A. Look at the map of expeditioners' routes below. Circle the following.

1. Grand Canyon   **2.** Snake River   **3.** Pikes Peak   **4.** Platte River

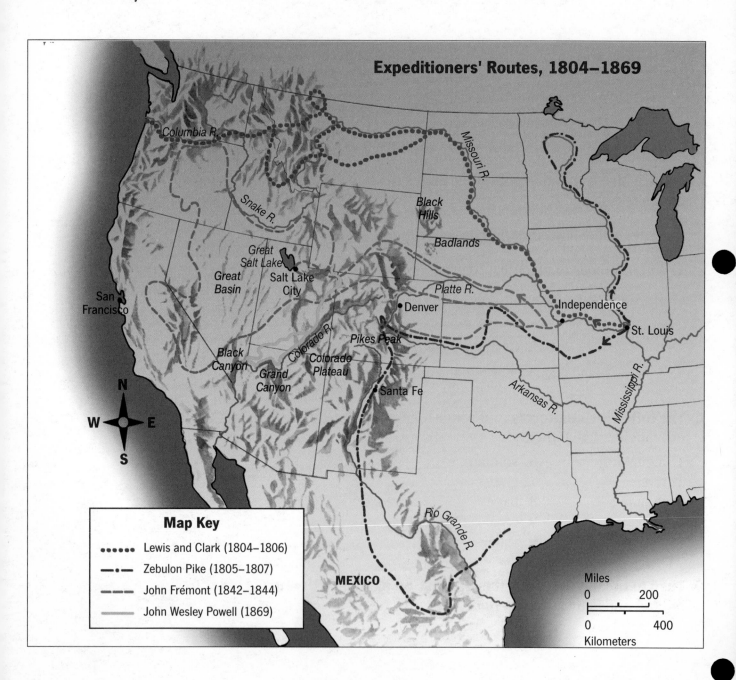

Expeditioners' Routes, 1804–1869

Map Key

- •••••• Lewis and Clark (1804–1806)
- –•–•– Zebulon Pike (1805–1807)
- – – – John Frémont (1842–1844)
- ——— John Wesley Powell (1869)

B. The map shows the routes of four famous expeditioners who went West. Using the map, answer the following questions.

1. Which explorer circled the land around the Great Basin?

   _____

2. Which explorer traveled up the Arkansas River into the mountains, and then crossed the Rio Grande twice?

   _____

3. Choose one of the explorers listed on the map key. Write a description of the route he followed. What kinds of landforms did the explorer encounter?

   _____

   _____

C. Physical features can be used as boundaries when dividing land. Suppose you were a settler traveling westward in the mid-1800s.

1. Choose a destination for your trip.

   _____

2. What route would you follow to arrive at your destination?

   _____

3. What kind of land features might you find along the way?

   _____

   _____

4. How might you use the land where you settle?

   _____

   _____

5. Your wagon train has a total of 30 wagons, each containing one family. Devise a method for dividing the land where you will settle. What boundaries will surround each family's plot of land? How will you decide what boundaries to use?

   _____

   _____

   _____

MAP SKILLS

Maps show where places are located. The political boundaries of countries, states, and cities are usually included on maps. The dots on a map usually designate cities. A star usually designates a capital city.

Map Key

★ Capitals   ⌇ Rivers

● Cities   ⌐ Boundaries

▨ Mountains

EUROPE

FINLAND

NORWAY

SWEDEN

RUSSIA

Oslo ★

ESTONIA

SCOTLAND

LATVIA

North Sea

DENMARK

LITHUANIA

IRELAND   ENGLAND

Copenhagen ★

Baltic Sea

ESTONIA

Thames River

BELARUS

Elbe River

NETHERLANDS

N

BELGIUM

GERMANY

POLAND

W ← → E

Rhine River

Dresden ●

S

LUXEMBOURG

Seine River

CZECH REPUBLIC

UKRAINE

Carpathian Mountains

Atlantic Ocean

Danube River

SLOVAKIA

Zurich ●

Munich ●

MOLDOVA

FRANCE

SWITZERLAND

AUSTRIA

HUNGARY

ROMANIA

THE ALPS

SLOVENIA

Milan ● Po River

CROATIA

Pyrenees Mountains

BOSNIA HERZEGOVINA

Danube River

PORTUGAL

YUGOSLAVIA

BULGARIA

Black Sea

SPAIN

Mediterranean Sea

ITALY

Adriatic Sea

MACEDONIA

TURKEY

ALBANIA

GREECE

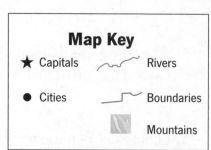

74

A. Look at the map of Europe. Circle the following cities and study their locations.

1. Zurich, Switzerland
2. Munich, Germany
3. Oslo, Norway
4. Copenhagen, Denmark
5. Dresden, Germany

B. Answer the following questions about the cities listed above.

1. Which of the five cities are landlocked? _____

2. What large bodies of water are the remaining two cities located near? _____

_____

3. Between the two cities located near large bodies of water, which would you consider to be the

most favorably located? _____

4. Why is the location of this city a favorable location? _____

_____

_____

C. Analyze and indicate each city's location on the chart below. Then indicate on the chart the advantages and disadvantages of cities being located close to or far from these features.

Cities	Location	Advantages	Disadvantages
Zurich, Switzerland			
Munich, Germany			
Oslo, Norway			
Copenhagen, Denmark			
Dresden, Germany			

Map Skills Using Maps to Learn About Population

A **census** is a count of the people living in the United States. It is done every ten years. **Population density** means the concentration of people living in a particular area. The map below uses colors to show the population density of Hawaii according to the 2000 census.

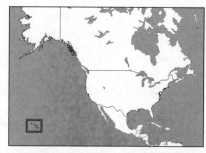

Population Density of the Hawaiian Islands

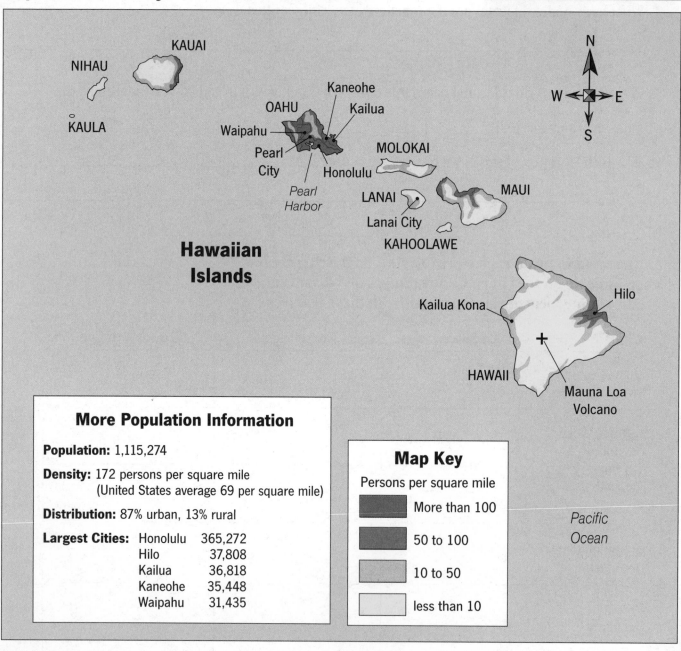

KAUAI

NIHAU

KAULA

OAHU

Kaneohe

Kailua

Waipahu

Pearl City

Honolulu

Pearl Harbor

MOLOKAI

LANAI

Lanai City

MAUI

KAHOOLAWE

Hawaiian Islands

Kailua Kona

Hilo

HAWAII

Mauna Loa Volcano

N W E S

More Population Information

Population: 1,115,274

Density: 172 persons per square mile
(United States average 69 per square mile)

Distribution: 87% urban, 13% rural

Largest Cities:

Honolulu	365,272
Hilo	37,808
Kailua	36,818
Kaneohe	35,448
Waipahu	31,435

Map Key

Persons per square mile

More than 100	
50 to 100	
10 to 50	
less than 10	

Pacific Ocean

A. Look at the map and answer the questions below.

1. List the nine islands that make up the state of Hawaii.

   a. _____   f. _____

   b. _____   g. _____

   c. _____   h. _____

   d. _____   i. _____

   e. _____

2. Which color on the map represents the highest density, or concentration of people?

   _____

3. Which color represents the sparsely populated areas—areas with the fewest people?

   _____

B. *Urban* **means "in, of, or like a city."** *Rural* **means "in, of, or like the country." Use the map to answer the following questions.**

1. Which map color would you say best represents urban areas? _____

2. Which color would you say best represents rural areas? _____

3. How many people per square mile live on the northern tip of the

   island of Hawaii? _____

4. How do the coasts of the islands compare to the inland areas in population?

   _____

5. Which Hawaiian island has the highest population? _____

6. On which island are most of the cities located? _____

7. Compare the city locations with the population density and note your

   observations. _____

   _____

77

MAP SKILLS   Using a Map to Compare Population Densities

Population maps can show population density, or how many people live in an area. While the figures on the number of Native Americans who lived long ago are only rough estimates, a population map can be used to show the approximate number of people who live in a region per square mile. This map compares the density of Native American populations in different regions of North America at the time the Europeans arrived. Look in the Almanac for information on different population terms.

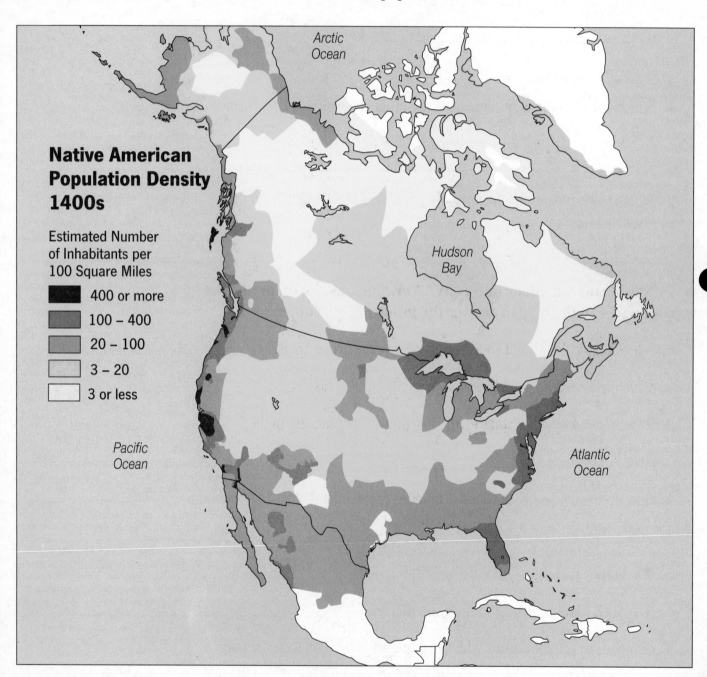

Native American Population Density 1400s

Estimated Number of Inhabitants per 100 Square Miles

- 400 or more
- 100 – 400
- 20 – 100
- 3 – 20
- 3 or less

Arctic Ocean

Hudson Bay

Pacific Ocean

Atlantic Ocean

A. Turn to the map of North America on page 4 in the Almanac. Notice the physical features of the following regions of the United States:

Northwest—the Pacific Ocean and many rivers filled with fish, mountains thick with forests that provided timber for shelter and animals for food.

Southwest—mostly desert with deep canyons and mountains; sun-baked soil provided raw material for shelters.

Eastern Woodlands—dense with trees, rivers, swamps, and animal life.

Great Plains—tall, vast grasslands provided home for roaming buffalo, which were a source of food, clothing, and shelter.

Circle and label these four regions on the map on page 78.

B. Compare the color patterns for high and low population densities on the map.

1. Which color represents a low population density? _____

2. Which color represents a high population density? _____

3. Which areas of the United States had a low population density? _____

_____

4. Which areas of the United States had a high population density? _____

_____

_____

C. Explain why some areas in the United States might have had an especially high population density. Base your answer on what you know about the geography and natural resources of the four regions prior to the time of Columbus.

_____

_____

_____

_____

_____

_____

MAP SKILLS

Using a Map to Find Location in Latitude and Longitude

Lines of latitude and longitude are drawn on a map to help us identify a place's specific location on the Earth's surface. These lines are measured in **degrees**, indicated by the ° symbol. Lines of latitude and longitude are expressed in numbers, often called coordinates.

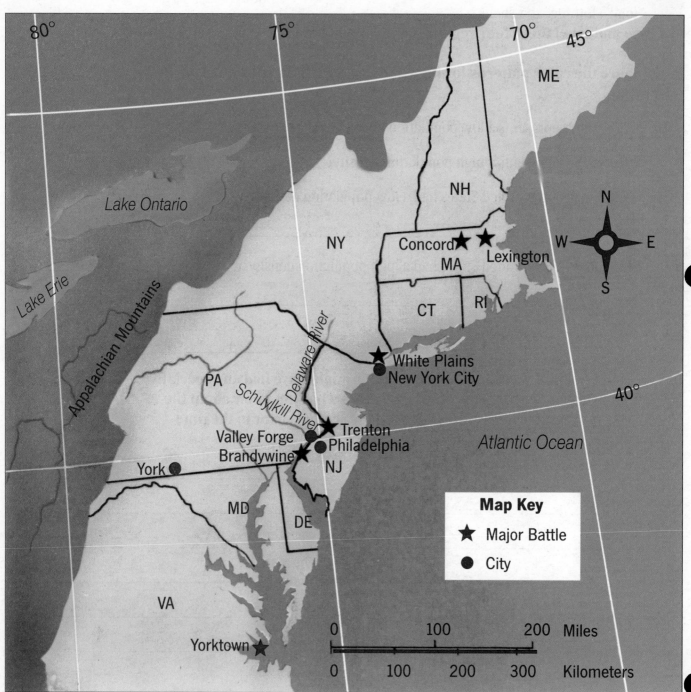

A. Use the map to answer the following questions about specific location.

1. What city lies at a latitude of 41°N and a longitude of 74°W?

   _____

2. About how many degrees of latitude are there between Philadelphia and New

   York City? _____

   _____

3. About how many degrees of longitude are there between White Plains, New York

   and York, Pennsylvania? _____

4. The Schuylkill River lies between what lines of latitude? _____

B. Look at the entire area that the map shows and answer the following questions.

1. About how many degrees of longitude does the map cover? _____

2. About how many degrees of latitude does the map cover? _____

C. Using the map, identify the places described below and answer the following questions.

1. If point A is located at 42°N and 75°W and point B is located at 40°N and 74°W, in what direction would you travel to get from point A to point B?

   _____

2. Is there a city at 39°N and 74°W? If so, what city is it?

   _____

3. About how many degrees of latitude are there between Yorktown, Virginia, and Philadelphia, Pennsylvania?

   _____

4. What are the latitude and longitude coordinates for Lexington, Massachusetts?

   _____

5. What are the latitude and longitude coordinates for York, Pennsylvania?

   _____

Map Skills

Using Latitude and Longitude to Find a Location

Latitude and longitude lines are horizontal and vertical lines drawn on a map to help you find and describe places on Earth. Lines of latitude are horizontal lines that circle the globe from east to west. Lines of longitude are vertical lines that extend from north to south on the globe. Lines of latitude and longitude provide the absolute location of a place.

The Voyage of Christopher Columbus, 1492

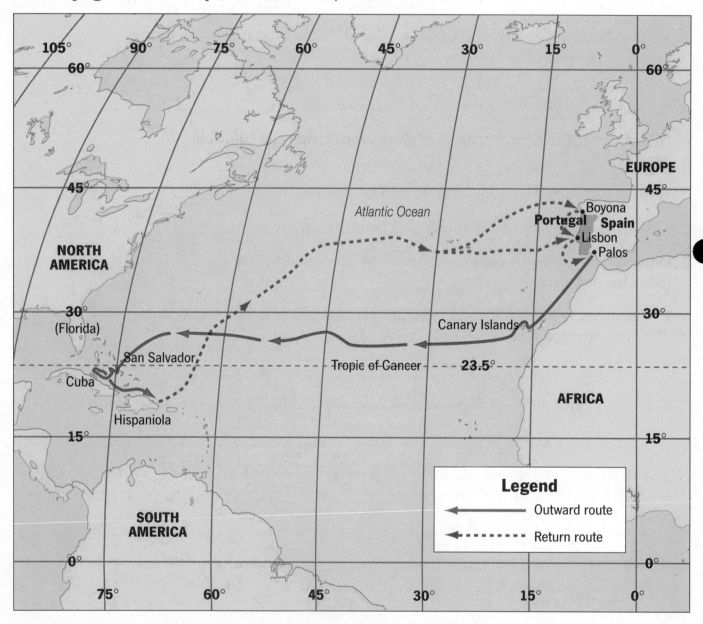

A. Look at the map of Columbus' travels in 1492 and answer the following questions.

1. Columbus left Palos, Spain, on August 3, 1492. What is the approximate latitude of Palos, Spain?

   _____

2. What is the approximate longitude of Palos, Spain? _____

3. What are the approximate latitude and longitude of the Canary Islands, where Columbus stopped in August 1492?

   _____   _____

4. If Columbus was at 30°N latitude and 60°W longitude, where would he be?

   _____

5. At about what latitude was Columbus when he landed on San Salvador?

   _____

6. Just south of San Salvador is a line of latitude with a special name. It is the northern boundary of the tropical region. What is this line of latitude called?

   _____

7. If Columbus had landed at 30°N latitude on the North American continent, where would he have landed?

   _____

B. Looking at the map, number the following events of Columbus' journey in the correct order. Beside each different place where Columbus stopped, write its latitude and longitude.

Sequence	Events	Latitude and Longitude
	Columbus lands at San Salvador Island.	
	The Santa Maria goes aground on a reef.	
	Two ships return to Palos.	
	The Niña and Pinta begin their return voyage.	
	Columbus reaches the Canary Islands.	
	Columbus sails three ships out of port Palos, Spain.	

83

MAP SKILLS

Using a Map to Determine Distance, Direction, and Time

Earth has been divided into 24 time zones. Each time zone forms a belt of longitude (15° across) in which most areas have the same local time. When you cross from one time zone to another, the local time changes by one hour. If you are traveling east, you add one hour for each time zone crossed. If you are traveling west, you subtract one hour for each time zone crossed.

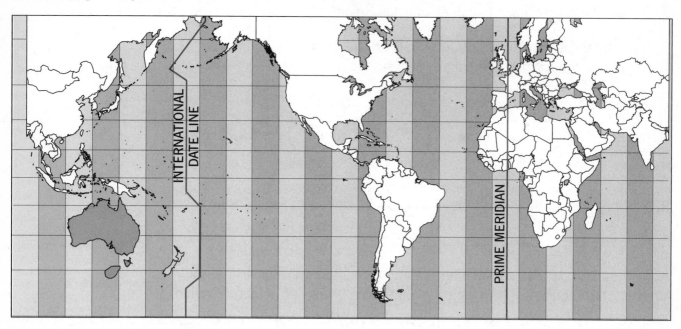

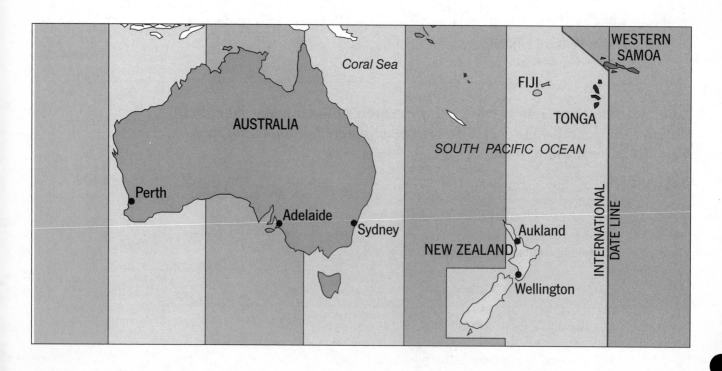

A. Use the time zone map to answer the following questions.

1. How many time zones are there in Australia?

_____

2. If it is 10 P.M. in Sydney, what time is it in Perth?

_____

3. How many time zones are there in New Zealand?

_____

4. If it is 10 P.M. in Sydney, what time is it in Wellington, New Zealand?

_____

The **international date line** is an imaginary line at 180° longitude that runs through the middle of the Pacific Ocean. By international agreement, it marks the spot where each new calendar day begins. Any time you cross the date line going from west to east, you move into the previous day (subtract one day). Anytime you cross the international date line going from east to west, you move into the following day (add one day). The time of day does not change. If you reach the date line at 4 P.M. on Tuesday coming from the east, it will be 4 P.M. Wednesday after you cross the line. If you cross back two hours later, it will be 6 P.M. on Tuesday.

B. With the previous information and the following scenario in mind, answer the questions below.

You are traveling from Western Samoa to Wellington, New Zealand. The trip takes four hours. You begin your trip at 7 A.M. on Saturday.

1. In which direction will you be traveling?

_____

2. How many time zones will you cross during your trip?

_____

3. Is New Zealand east or west of the international date line?

_____

4. What day and time will you arrive in Wellington, New Zealand?

_____

MAP SKILLS
Using a Map to Look at Boundaries

Forces that shaped North America long ago created many of the boundaries between countries today. A **boundary** is an imaginary line that divides two states or countries. Physical features, such as mountains, that divide land are **natural boundaries.** Boundaries not formed by a physical feature are **artificial boundaries.**

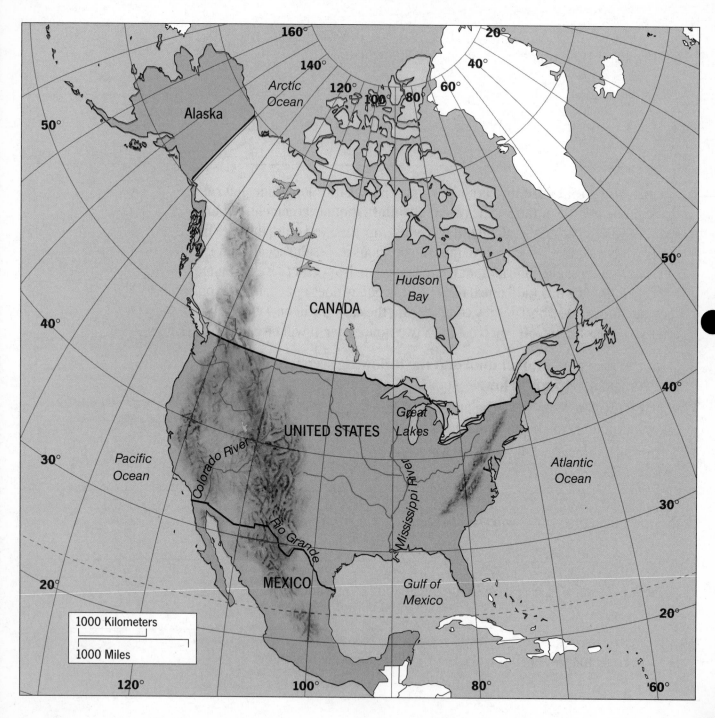

A. Look at the map of North America and answer the following questions.

1. What are the three countries of North America?

_____

_____

_____

2. What name is used to refer to the five lakes that form a boundary between

Canada and the United States? _____

Is it a natural or artificial boundary? _____

3. Name the river that forms a boundary between Mexico and the

United States. _____

Is it a natural or artificial boundary? _____

4. Name the area of land that is on the northwestern boundary of Canada and the

country that owns that land. _____

Is this a natural or artificial boundary? _____

5. What is the number of the parallel line that forms a long section of the

boundary between Canada and the United States? _____

Is this a natural or artificial boundary? _____

B. Look at the coastline boundaries of North America and complete the following questions.

1. What ocean borders the east side of the United States and Canada? _____

2. What ocean borders the west side of North America? _____

3. What ocean is north of Canada? _____

4. What large body of water lies between Mexico and the Atlantic Ocean? _____

C. Draw some conclusions about the above information.

1. What does the map of North America tell you about boundaries? _____

_____

2. Why do you think waterways are common boundaries in North America? _____

_____

Maps that show boundary lines are called **political maps.** Political maps can show cities, towns, highways, and sometimes other features such as ferry routes, agricultural areas, and military bases. Political maps can also show international boundaries between different countries.

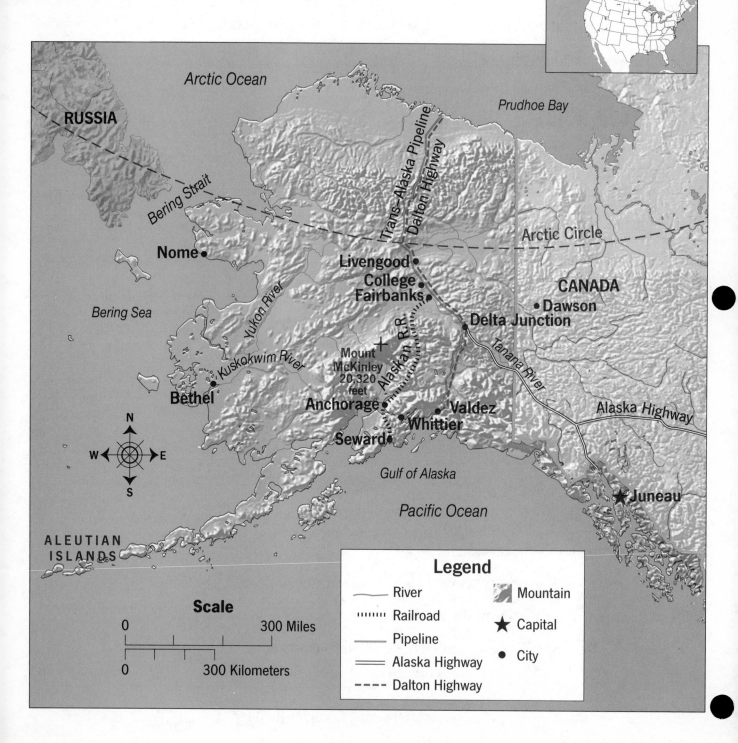

Arctic Ocean

Prudhoe Bay

RUSSIA

Trans-Alaska Pipeline

Dalton Highway

Bering Strait

Arctic Circle

Nome

Livengood

College

Fairbanks

CANADA

Dawson

Delta Junction

Bering Sea

Yukon River

Kuskokwim River

Mount McKinley 20,320 feet

Alaskan R.R.

Tanana River

Alaska Highway

Bethel

Anchorage

Valdez

Whittier

Alaska Highway

Seward

Gulf of Alaska

Juneau

Pacific Ocean

ALEUTIAN ISLANDS

N
W   E
S

Legend

—— River		Mountain
······· Railroad		★ Capital
—— Pipeline		● City
══ Alaska Highway		
- - - Dalton Highway		

Scale

0   300 Miles

0   300 Kilometers

A. Look at the map and identify the following features.

1. Find an international boundary line and trace it with a red line.

2. Find the highway line and trace it with a yellow line.

3. Find the railroad line and trace it with a blue line.

4. Find the Trans-Alaska Pipeline and trace it with a green line.

B. Look at the legend on the map. Find these symbols and write what each one stands for.

1. '''''''' _____

2. —— _____

3. - - - - _____

4. ⌒ _____

C. Use the map to answer these questions about international boundaries.

1. What country borders the east side of Alaska? _____

2. How can you tell the boundary line between Alaska and that country?

_____

3. What country borders the west side of Alaska? _____

4. What body of water forms a boundary between Alaska and that country? _____

_____

D. Think about the boundaries between Alaska and Canada and Alaska and Russia. Write a few sentences explaining which is a physical boundary and which is a human boundary. Explain your answer.

_____

_____

_____

MAP SKILLS

Using a Map to Locate Natural and Human Features

Maps often show physical features, such as landforms and bodies of water. Maps can also show human features—exploration routes and places that people explored, settled, and named.

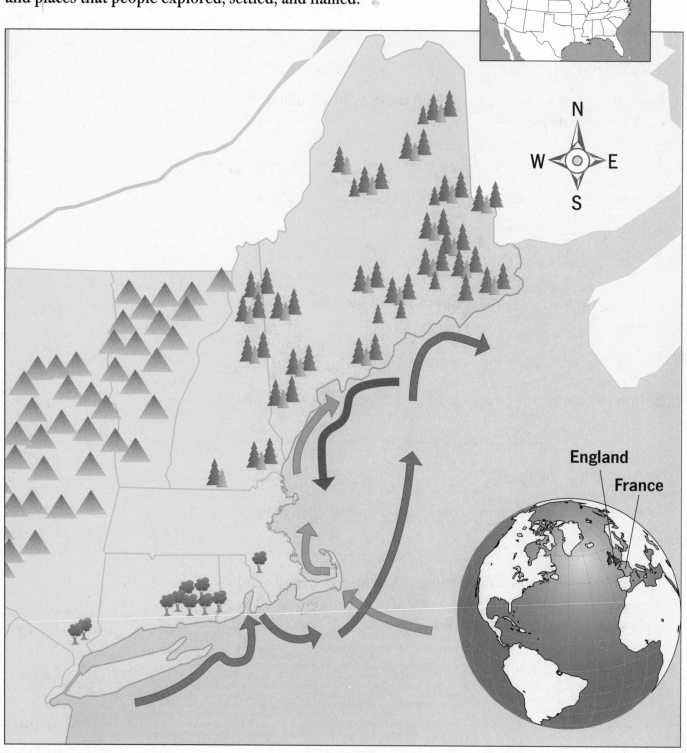

A. List the six states shown on the map that make up the New England region. Then label them on the map.

1. _____   4. _____

2. _____   5. _____

3. _____   6. _____

B. Use information from the Internet or your local library and the Almanac to identify the following. After you identify these places, locate and label them on the map.

1. A name for the region of forests before European exploration

   _____

   Trace this region on the map.

2. The mountains of eastern North America that run through

   New England _____

   Draw these mountains on the map.

3. The ocean that the explorers crossed to get to North America _____

   Label this ocean on the map.

4. The country that sent Giovanni da Verrazano and Samuel de Champlain

   to explore coastal New England _____

   Draw a line from this country to the New England region on the globe.

5. The country that sent John Smith to explore coastal New England _____

   Draw a line from this country to the New England region on the globe.

6. The harbor that Champlain mapped and described _____

   Label this harbor on the map.

7. The harbor that John Smith mapped and described _____

   Label this harbor on the map.

MAP SKILLS

Using Maps to Compare Natural and Human-Made Features

Maps are created to show specific information such as roads, state borders, or physical features of the land. They can help us identify which physical features of the land are natural or human-made. These two kinds of physical features can be shown and compared on two maps.

Map A

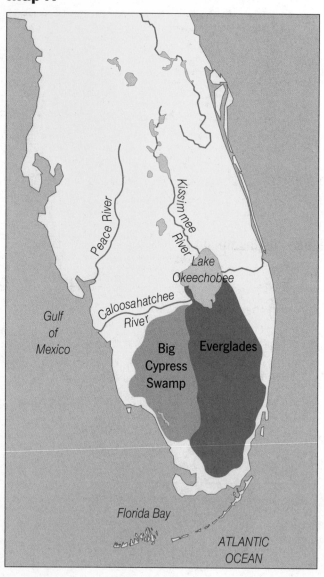

Map B

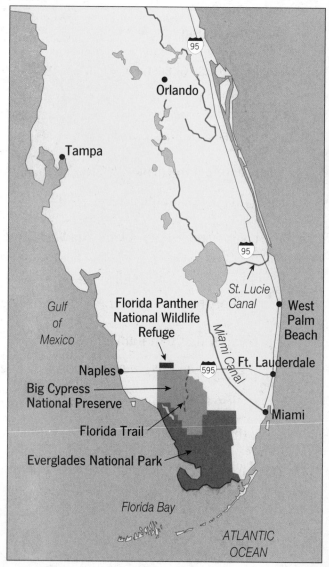

A. Look at the maps of southern Florida. Put an *X* on the following places on each map.

Map A
1. Lake Okeechobee
2. Big Cypress Swamp
3. Everglades
4. Kissimmee River

Map B
5. Florida Panther National Wildlife Refuge
6. Everglades National Park
7. Big Cypress National Preserve
8. Florida Trail

B. Use both maps to complete the following.

1. Indicate on which map you can find each of the following and whether each is natural or human-made.

   a. Big Cypress Swamp? _____

   b. Orlando? _____

   c. Big Cypress National Preserve? _____

   d. an interstate highway? _____

   e. a canal? _____

   f. rivers? _____

2. Look at Map B. Where are most of the cities located?

   _____

   _____

3. Draw the information from Map B onto Map A.
   a. Place the cities, roads, and canals on Map A.
   b. Add the boundaries to show Big Cypress National Preserve and Everglades National Park.
   c. Are any human-made features such as cities located inside Big Cypress

   National Preserve and Everglades National Park? _____

4. Now look at Map A. Describe how much of the Everglades and Big Cypress Swamp has been preserved by humans and what has happened to the remainder of the wetlands.

   _____

   _____

Map Skills

Locating Features on a Map

You can use a map to locate and look at important straits. The map below shows the important straits in southwest Asia and northern Africa. By studying the map you can see why the straits are important for trade and defense and how these narrow channels of water can affect relationships between places.

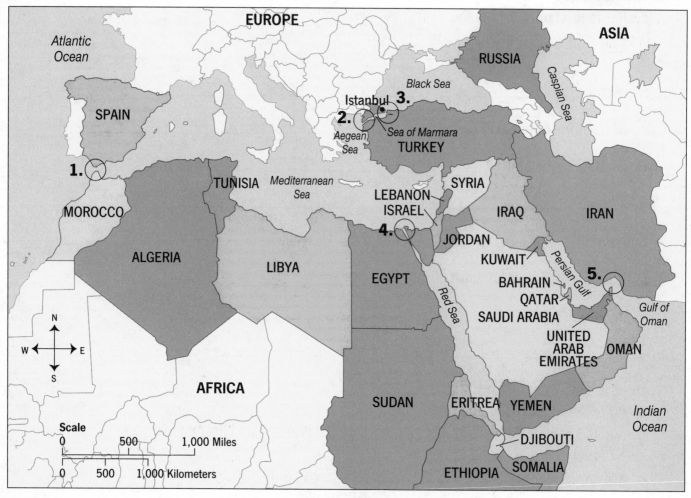

Map Index

1. Strait of Gibraltar
2. Dardanelles Strait
3. Bosporous Strait
4. Suez Canal
5. Strait of Hormuz

A. On the map locate the waterways listed below. Draw a symbol to represent a strait next to each one.

1. Bosporus Strait
2. Dardanelles Strait
3. Strait of Gibraltar
4. Strait of Hormuz
5. Suez Canal

B. Use the map and Almanac information on pages 2, 3 and 4 to answer the following questions.

1. Would shipping be easier to block in the Gibraltar or Bosporus strait? Why?

_____

_____

2. What countries rely on the Strait of Hormuz to ship their oil? _____

_____

_____

3. Why would Russia want control of the Bosporus Strait? _____

_____

_____

4. How is the Suez Canal different from the straits in this area of the world? _____

_____

5. Why is the Suez Canal important to Israel? _____

_____

6. How was the Strait of Hormuz important to the countries involved in the

    Persian Gulf War? _____

_____

_____

_____

7. Why has the Dardanelles Strait been important throughout history? _____

_____

_____

MAP SKILLS Using a Relief Map

The word *relief* refers to the high points and low points of a land area.
A **relief map** shows different altitudes, or elevations, of mountains.
It also shows the relief of valleys.

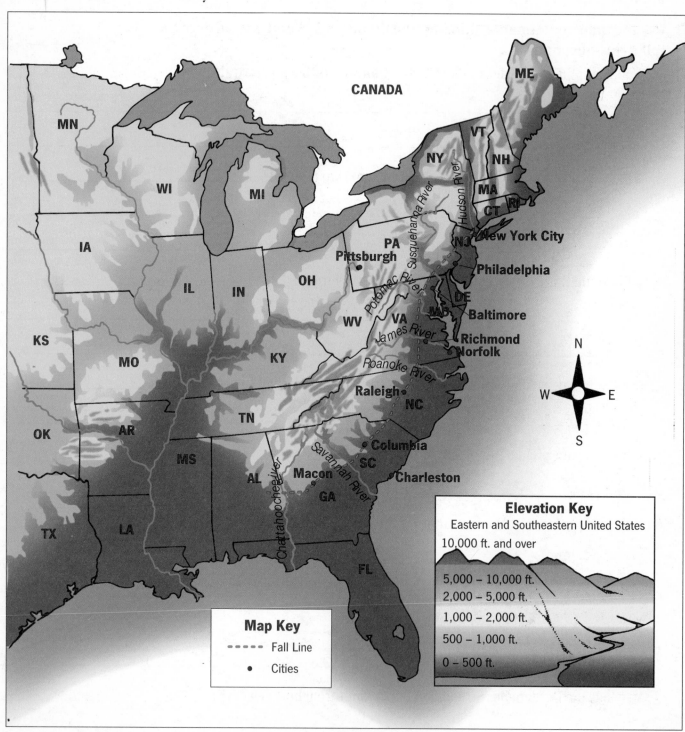

Elevation Key
Eastern and Southeastern United States
10,000 ft. and over

5,000 – 10,000 ft.
2,000 – 5,000 ft.
1,000 – 2,000 ft.
500 – 1,000 ft.
0 – 500 ft.

Map Key
----- Fall Line
• Cities

A. List the major cities along the fall line.

_____   _____

_____   _____

_____   _____

_____

B. Look at the map and write down the approximate elevations of the following cities.

1. Raleigh, North Carolina _____

2. Pittsburgh, Pennsylvania _____

3. Baltimore, Maryland _____

4. Columbia, South Carolina _____

C. Look at the fall line on the map. Answer the following questions.

1. Explain why Raleigh, Baltimore, and Columbia are fall line cities.

_____

_____

_____

2. Explain why Pittsburgh is not a fall line city.

_____

_____

_____

D. In the twentieth century, industry has developed in all regions of the United States. Explain why industry is no longer dependent on physical features such as the eastern fall line.

_____

_____

_____

_____

MAP SKILLS

Using an Elevation Key

We know that the land that a map shows us is not always flat. We use a map's **elevation key** to help us understand the shape of the land. **Elevation**, or **relief**, is measured in meters or feet. It is the height the land rises above sea level.

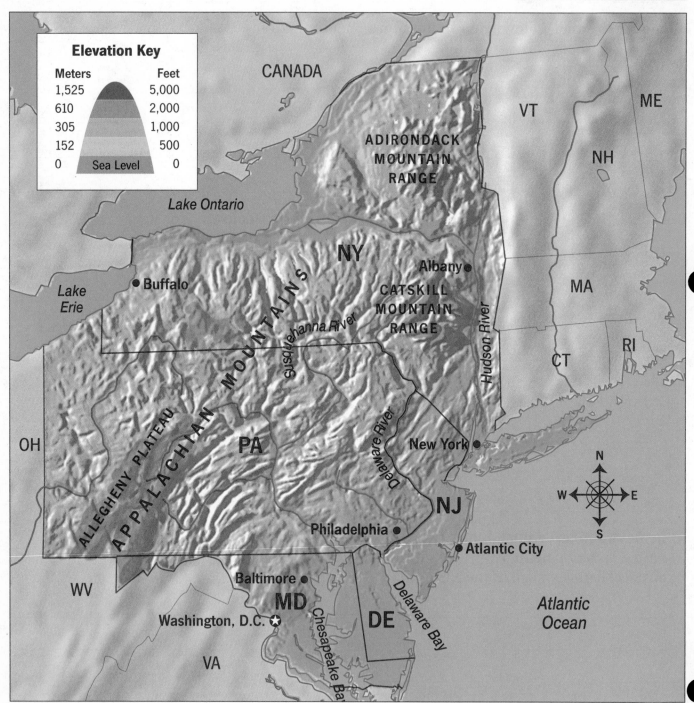

Elevation Key

Meters		Feet
1,525		5,000
610		2,000
305		1,000
152		500
0	Sea Level	0

CANADA

VT

ME

NH

ADIRONDACK
MOUNTAIN
RANGE

Lake Ontario

NY

Albany

MA

Buffalo

Lake
Erie

CATSKILL
MOUNTAIN
RANGE

Hudson River

RI

CT

Susquehanna River

APPALACHIAN MOUNTAINS

ALLEGHENY PLATEAU

OH

PA

Delaware River

New York

NJ

N
W E
S

Philadelphia

Atlantic City

WV

Baltimore

MD

Washington, D.C.

DE

Delaware Bay

Atlantic
Ocean

Chesapeake Bay

VA

A. Look at the elevation key to answer the following questions.

1. Write the elevation of the land shown in yellow.

   _____ meters   _____ feet

2. Which elevation is higher, the light green area or the orange area?

   _____

B. Look at the map of the Middle Atlantic region.

1. What is the elevation of most of the land along the Atlantic Ocean?

   _____

2. Describe how the land changes as you travel from west to east.

   _____

   _____

C. Find Buffalo, New York, on Lake Erie. Draw a line from west to east going from Buffalo to Albany, New York.

1. What two colors do you pass through? What are the elevations?

   a. Elevation color   **b.** Elevation in feet

   _____   _____

   _____   _____

2. What is the name of the mountain range north of the line that you drew?

   _____

3. Continue your line from Albany, New York, by tracing the Hudson River south

   to New York City. What is the elevation in feet? _____

4. Do you think the route from Buffalo to Albany was a good route for the

   Erie Canal? Why?

   _____

   _____

   _____

Map Skills

Using a Physical Map to Compare Continents

Topography shown on a map indicates the physical features of an area on Earth's surface. The elevation of mountain ranges, plains, plateaus, depressions, and basins can be identified by contour lines, shading, and color layers. In addition, physical maps show the shape of peninsulas, islands, lakes, coastlines, and borders.

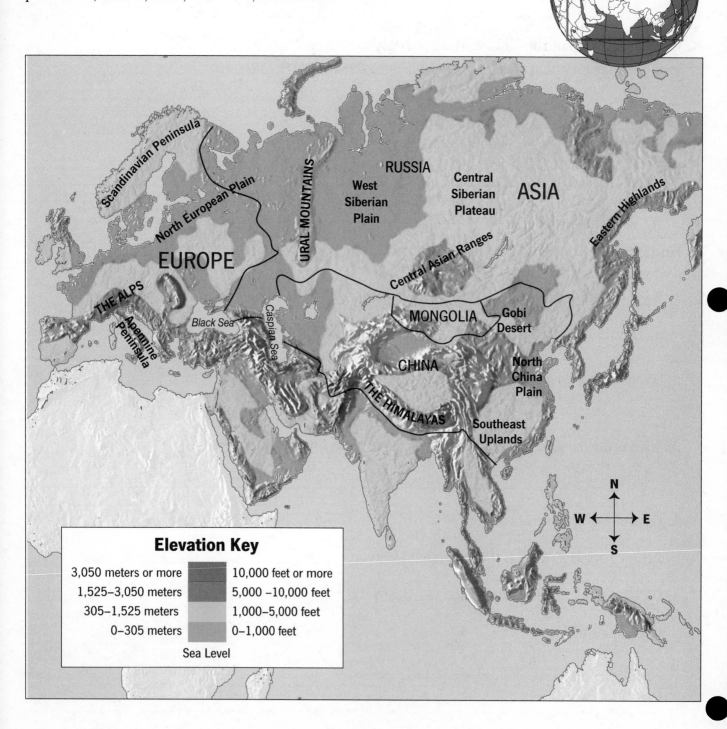

Elevation Key

3,050 meters or more	10,000 feet or more
1,525–3,050 meters	5,000 –10,000 feet
305–1,525 meters	1,000–5,000 feet
0–305 meters	0–1,000 feet

Sea Level

A. Study the elevation key on the map of Europe and Asia. Use the key and the map to help you identify the following features.

1. How did you use the map to help you identify:

   a. mountain ranges?

   _____

   b. plains?

   _____

2. Define and distinguish between a peninsula and an island.

   _____

   _____

B. Look at the map and complete the following.

1. Draw a line showing where Europe and Asia are divided.

2. Using the map, write a description of the physical features you see in Europe.

   _____

   _____

   _____

3. Why do you think Europe is considered a peninsula of Asia, rather than Asia being considered a peninsula of Europe?

   _____

4. Write a description of the physical features of Asia.

   _____

   _____

   _____

5. Describe the physical features that are shared by both Europe and Asia.

   _____

   _____

   _____

MAP SKILLS

Using a Map to Link Elevation, Climate, and Vegetation

Maps that show the boundaries of countries and states are called political maps. Political maps can also show locations of mountains, rivers, and lakes.

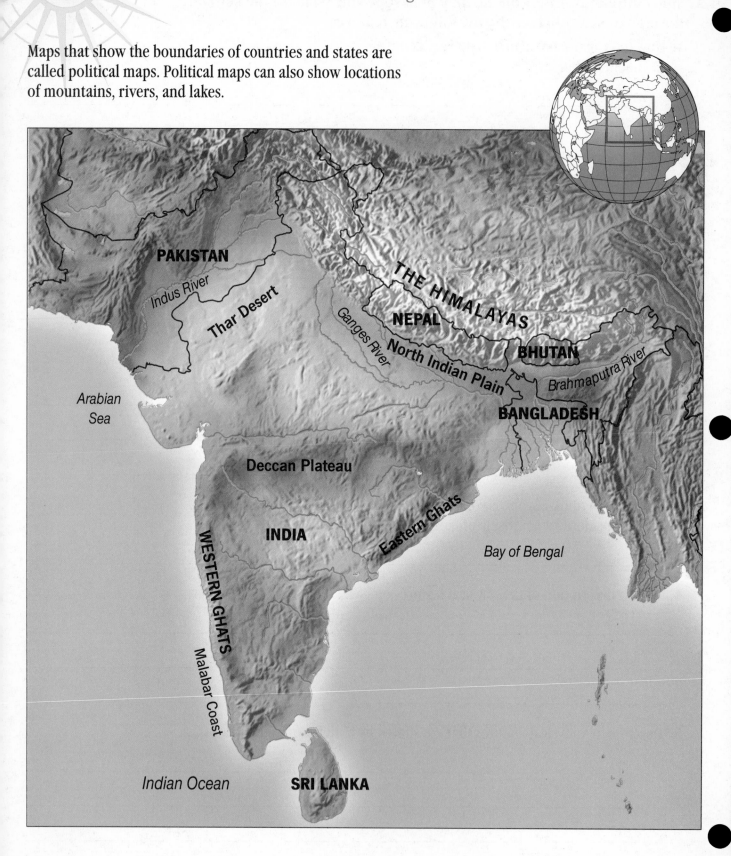

PAKISTAN

Indus River

Thar Desert

THE HIMALAYAS

NEPAL

Ganges River

North Indian Plain

BHUTAN

Brahmaputra River

BANGLADESH

Arabian Sea

Deccan Plateau

WESTERN GHATS

INDIA

Eastern Ghats

Bay of Bengal

Malabar Coast

Indian Ocean

SRI LANKA

A. Look at the political and physical map of south Asia and complete the following.

   1. List the six countries shown.

   _____   _____

   _____   _____

   _____   _____

   2. Name the three large bodies of water that border south Asia.

   _____

   3. What are the three major mountain ranges that surround India?

   _____

   4. What are the three main rivers in south Asia?

   _____

B. Look for the precipitation and vegetation maps of India in the Almanac. Precipitation maps show the amount of rainfall an area receives. Vegetation maps show how plant life responds to climactic conditions. Complete the following.

   1. Which parts of India receive the most rainfall?

   _____

   2. What type of vegetation is found in the areas with the most rainfall?

   _____

   3. Describe the general relationship between high levels of rainfall and vegetation.

   _____

C. Make connections among what you have learned about rainfall, vegetation, and physical features. Answer the following questions.

   1. What kinds of physical features are located on the western coast and north-eastern coasts of India?

   _____

   2. How do these physical features affect rainfall during the monsoon season?

   _____

   _____

MAP SKILLS

Using a Dot Map to Identify
Grain Belts of the Midwest

Maps can show where crops are grown. Maps can also show how much of
an area is planted with different crops. Knowing where a crop is grown
and how much of it is grown in an area helps you identify the "belt," or
zone, for that crop. Some areas of the Midwest are known as the Corn
Belt, the Winter Wheat Belt, and the Spring Wheat Belt.

Corn and Wheat Belts

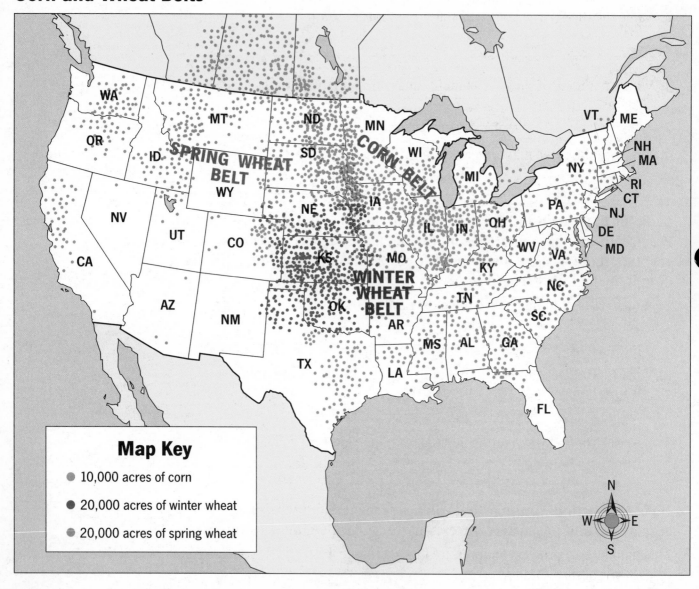

Map Key

- 10,000 acres of corn
- 20,000 acres of winter wheat
- 20,000 acres of spring wheat

A. Look at the map and circle the following.

   1. Illinois   3. Nebraska   5. Missouri

   2. Iowa   4. Arizona   6. Map key

B. Use the map and map key to answer the following questions.

   1. a. What does a red dot mean? _____

      b. What does a green dot mean? _____

   2. a. Name at least five states where corn is grown. _____

                                        _____

                                        _____

      b. How do you know corn is grown in the states you named? _____

                                          _____

C. Answer the following.

   1. How many dots do you see in Arizona? _____

   2. What color is each dot? _____

                                          _____

   3. How many acres of corn are grown in Arizona? _____

      How do you know? _____

   4. Is more corn grown in Arizona or Illinois? _____

      Explain how you know. _____

                                          _____

D. Write a few sentences comparing the amount of corn grown in Ohio to the amount of corn grown in Missouri.

_____

_____

_____

_____

MAP SKILLS

Using a Map to Look at Resources
of Early Settlements

The Spanish, English, and French settled areas of the present-day United States. The
Spanish created large ranches to maintain horses and mules for their silver and
gold mining work. The English settlers raised tobacco, corn, and other crops which
they then sold in Europe. The French settlers made a living by hunting small forest
animals whose fur they would sell to Europe for making garments.

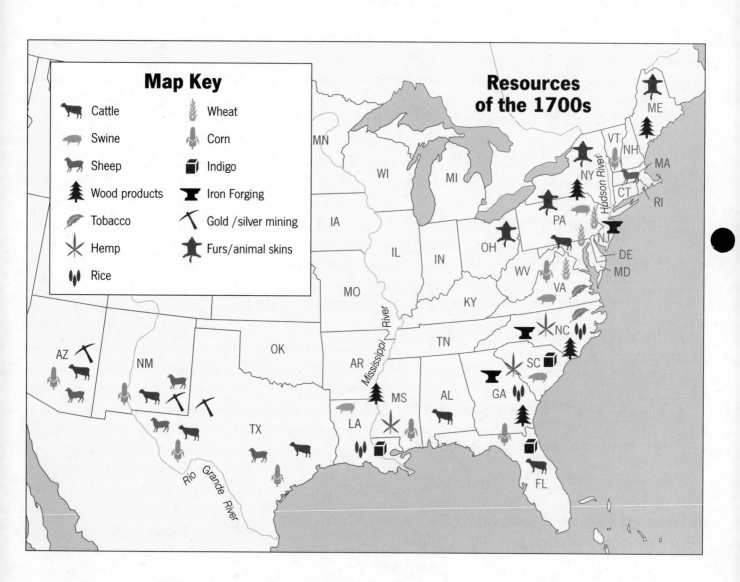

Map Key

Cattle		Wheat	
Swine		Corn	
Sheep		Indigo	
Wood products		Iron Forging	
Tobacco		Gold / silver mining	
Hemp		Furs/animal skins	
Rice			

Resources of the 1700s

1. Name two farm products raised in the 1700s by settlers from each of the following countries.

   a. England _____   _____

   b. France _____   _____

   c. Spain _____   _____

2. Some of the resources the settlers found did not have to be grown, but still came from the land. These types of resources are raw materials. Name two kinds of raw materials found in the 1700s by settlers from each of the following countries.

   a. England _____   _____

   b. France _____   _____

   c. Spain _____   _____

3. List below each of the products you named above and how Europeans and Native Americans might have used these farm products.

Farm Products	European Uses	Native American Uses

4. Which group of early colonists relied most heavily on farming? _____

5. Which group of early settlers relied most heavily on the land's raw materials? _____

6. Do you think the Spanish, French, and English settlers used more of the products they raised in North America or traded more with their native countries? Explain your answer.

_____

_____

MAP SKILLS
Using a Map to Find
Where a Crop Is Grown

The map below uses shades of color to represent the different wheat belts in North America. The northern wheat belt is the spring wheat belt. Wheat is planted in the spring and harvested in the fall. The southern wheat belt is the winter wheat belt. Wheat is planted in the fall and harvested in the spring.

Wheat-Producing Areas of North America

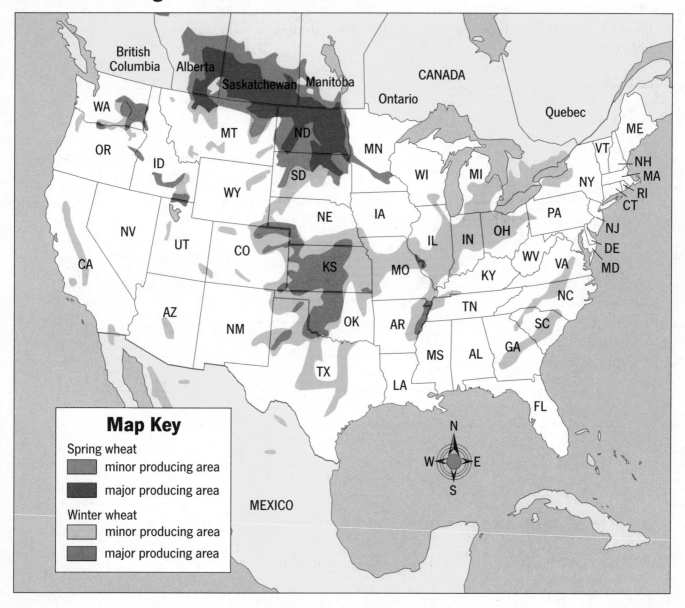

A. Look at the map and complete the following.

    1. Underline the names of the states in the northern spring wheat belt.

    2. Circle the names of the states in the southern winter wheat belt.

B. Answer the following questions about where the different kinds of wheat are grown.

    1. Which two states grow the most wheat? _____

    _____

    2. Which states produce both spring and winter wheat? _____

    _____

    _____

    3. Which states are minor producers of winter wheat? _____

    _____

    _____

    _____

    _____

    4. Is there more winter wheat or spring wheat grown in the United States? _____

    _____

    5. Which three spring wheat producing states grow the smallest amount of spring wheat?

    _____

    _____

    _____

    6. Where in North America is the most spring wheat grown?

    _____

    _____

MAP SKILLS

Using a Map to Identify Resources in an Area

The government in Uganda changed the natural balance in Lake Victoria for economic reasons. The decision to add a new species of fish to the lake has resulted in one of the worst possible outcomes. The Nile perch have almost depleted a major food source that many Ugandans and Kenyans have relied on for years. Study the map to decide how other resources might be used to benefit the Lake Victoria people and economy.

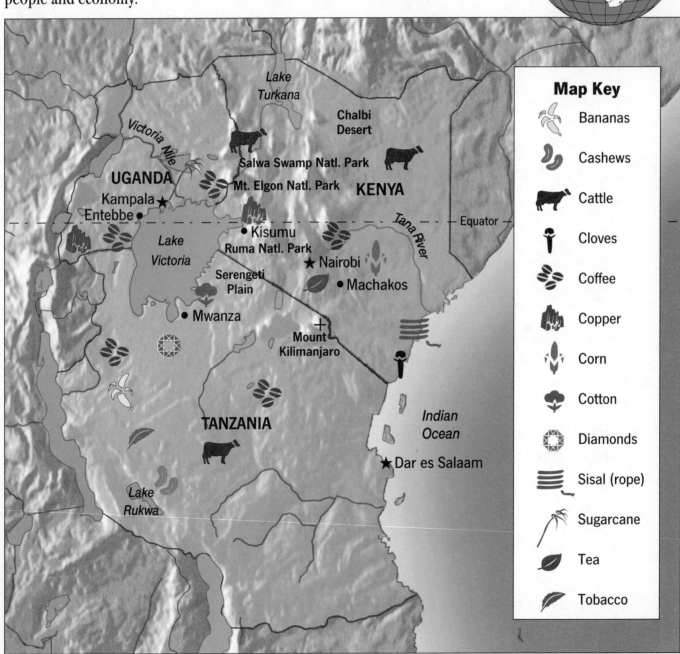

Map Key

- Bananas
- Cashews
- Cattle
- Cloves
- Coffee
- Copper
- Corn
- Cotton
- Diamonds
- Sisal (rope)
- Sugarcane
- Tea
- Tobacco

A. Using the map legend, make a list of the resources found in the area of Kenya near Lake Victoria. Remember that resources can include crops, animals, minerals, and natural features that might promote tourism.

_____   _____

_____   _____

_____   _____

_____   _____

B. Think about the resources found in the Lake Victoria area and answer the following questions.

1. The land used for farming around Lake Victoria is very dry. When there is no rain, crops such as corn will not grow, and the people have no food. What available resource could farmers use to water their corn in times of low rainfall? How would they transport the resource?

_____

_____

2. Nile perch were added to Lake Victoria so the area would have a product that could be exported. Describe alternative ways that people might have improved the economy of the area.

_____

_____

_____

_____

3. List advantages and disadvantages for each of your answers to question 2.

_____

_____

_____

_____

_____

_____

MAP SKILLS   Using a Map Scale to Figure Out Distance

In the fifteenth century explorers traveled by ship along the coast of Africa. Today, some of the cities where technological discoveries are being made are along the east coast of the United States. We can use a map scale to figure out the distance by water and land between some of the cities.

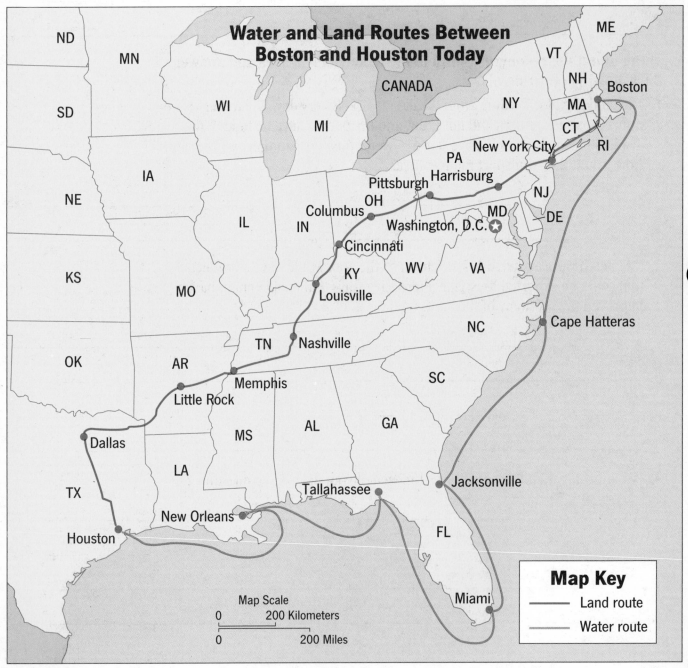

Water and Land Routes Between Boston and Houston Today

ND
MN
SD
WI
MI
CANADA
ME
VT
NH
NY
MA
CT
Boston
New York City
RI
IA
PA
Harrisburg
Pittsburgh
OH
Columbus
NJ
DE
MD
Washington, D.C.
IN
Cincinnati
WV
VA
KY
Louisville
KS
MO
NC
Cape Hatteras
TN
Nashville
OK
AR
SC
Memphis
Little Rock
AL
GA
Dallas
MS
LA
Tallahassee
Jacksonville
TX
New Orleans
FL
Houston
Miami

Map Scale
0   200 Kilometers
0   200 Miles

Map Key
— Land route
— Water route

112

A. Use the map scale to answer the following questions.

1. How many miles are represented on the scale?

_____

2. Using a ruler and the map scale to determine the distance, approximately
how many miles by air is Boston from New York City?

_____

**B. Use a piece of string and a ruler to measure the distance by water between
Boston and Cape Hatteras on the map and answer the following questions.**

1. How many inches is the length of string that represents the distance from Boston

to Cape Hatteras? _____ inch(es)

2. Measure the miles line on the map scale. Complete the following.

_____ inch(es) is equal to _____ miles.

3. How many miles by water is Boston from Cape Hatteras? _____

**C. Use a string and the map scale to measure and determine the distance
of the land and water routes between Boston and Houston.**

1. How long is the land route from Boston to Houston? _____

2. How long is the water route from Boston to Houston? _____

3. If you had been traveling in the 1400s from what is now Boston to what is now
Houston, which route would you have taken? Think about the ways people traveled
during that time. Explain your answer.

_____

_____

_____

4. If you were traveling from Boston to Houston in the 1990s, would you take
the water or land route? Explain why.

_____

_____

_____

_____

MAP SKILLS

The map shown below can help you figure out a journey route that goes through the desert.

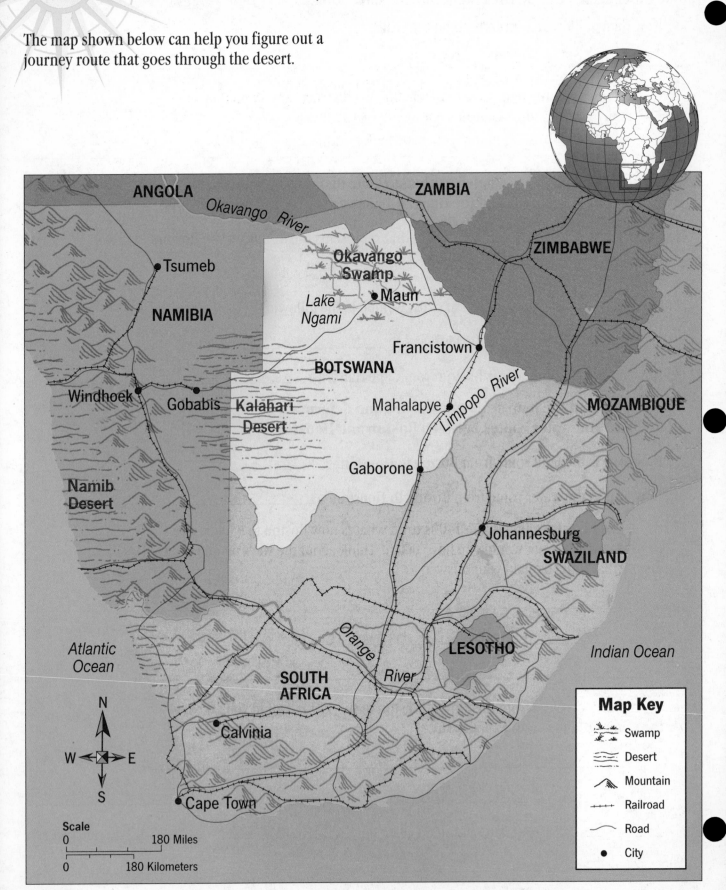

Map Key
- ~ Swamp
- ~ Desert
- ⌃ Mountain
- ┼┼┼ Railroad
- ~ Road
- • City

Scale
0 — 180 Miles
0 — 180 Kilometers

A. Study the map. Using different colored pencils for each item listed below, circle the following on the map.

1. Windhoek, Namibia and Gabarone, Botswana
2. Kalahari Desert
3. Towns or settlements along the northern route between Windhoek and Gabarone

B. Use the map, scale, and legend to complete the following.

1. If you were flying from Windhoek directly to Gabarone, how many miles would you travel?

_____

2. What other two methods of transportation could be used to get from Windhoek to Gabarone? In different colors, trace these two routes on your map.

_____

3. What form of transportation and route would be the quickest and easiest to travel from Windhoek to Gabarone, and how many miles would the route be?

_____

_____

_____

4. Describe the physical features you would encounter as you travel from east to west.

_____

5. What supplies would you need to take with you on your trip using the quickest and easiest route? Explain your answer.

_____

_____

_____

6. What form of transportation and route would be the longest and hardest to travel from Windhoek to Gabarone, and how many miles would the route be?

_____

_____

_____

MAP SKILLS Using Thematic Maps

In the Pacific Northwest warm, moist air moves in from the Pacific Ocean. As the air reaches the land, it flows up over the Coastal Range of mountains. It then flows down and across the Willamette Valley until it reaches a second, higher range of mountains, the Cascades. Look at the map below.

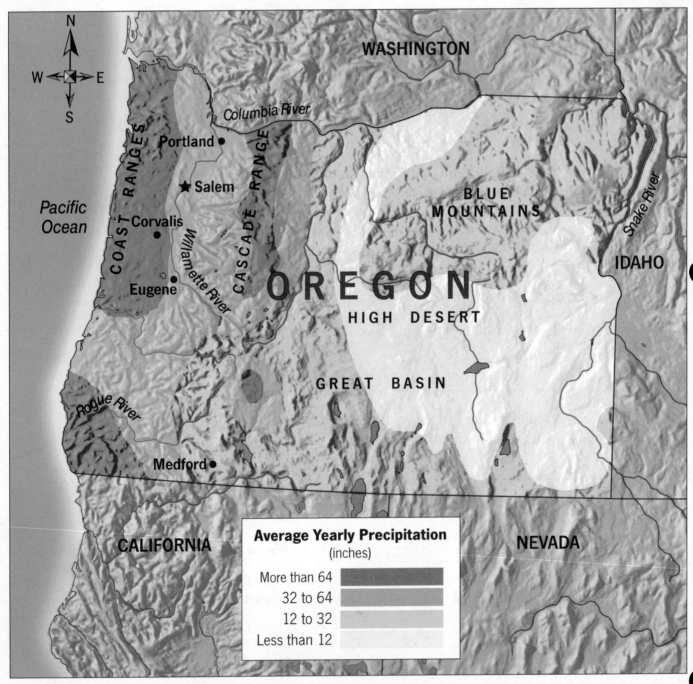

Average Yearly Precipitation
(inches)

More than 64
32 to 64
12 to 32
Less than 12

A. Study the map and the precipitation key.

1. What areas have the highest average precipitation? _____

2. What physical features are found in or near the areas that have the highest

   precipitation? _____

3. What areas show the lowest average precipitation? _____

   _____

4. What physical features are found in the areas that have the lowest

   precipitation? _____

B. The occurrence of heavy rainfall in western Oregon and dry climate in eastern Oregon
is due to *orographic precipitation*, which occurs when warm air is forced upward by a
rise in land, such as a hill or mountain. As the warm air rises and meets the cool air
over the mountain, precipitation is released and the air becomes dry before traveling
down the other side. Draw a diagram of this process in the appropriate place on the
map on page 116 .

1. What happens to the air as it moves up the ocean side of the mountain?

   _____

   _____

2. Where does it rain? _____

   _____

3. What is the air like as it moves down the far side of the mountain?

   _____

   _____

MAP SKILLS   Using a Legend to Identify Ocean Depth

Maps that show ocean depth can help us find out where a tsunami might form and how dangerous it might become. Most tsunamis originate in the trenches, or the deepest parts, of the Pacific Ocean. Scientists can measure how fast a tsunami is moving based on the depth of the sea through which it travels.

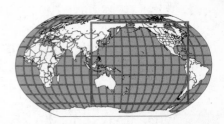

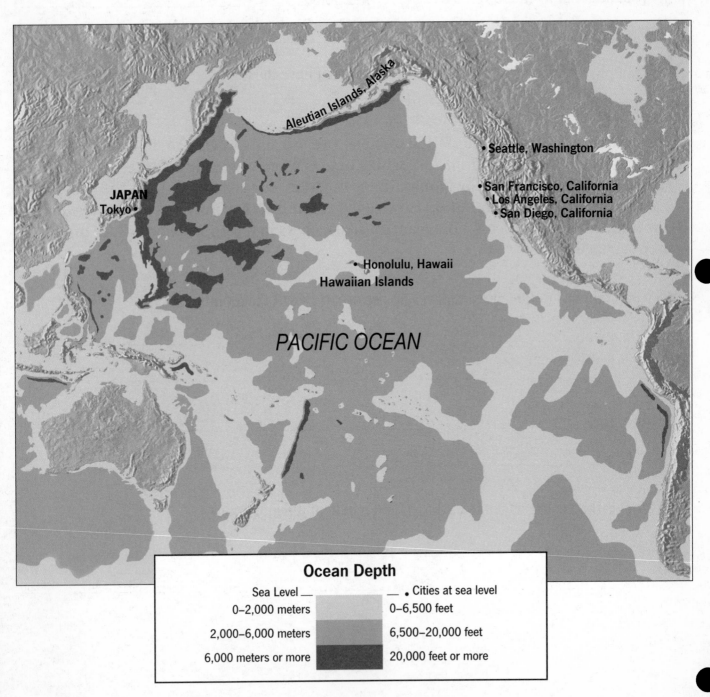

Aleutian Islands, Alaska

• Seattle, Washington

• San Francisco, California
• Los Angeles, California
• San Diego, California

JAPAN
Tokyo •

• Honolulu, Hawaii
Hawaiian Islands

PACIFIC OCEAN

Ocean Depth

Sea Level ———	——— • Cities at sea level
0–2,000 meters	0–6,500 feet
2,000–6,000 meters	6,500–20,000 feet
6,000 meters or more	20,000 feet or more

A. Maps show ocean depth and area at sea level. Study the map and legend and complete the following.

1. The cities on the map are at sea level, the place where land is the same height as the sea.

    a. List the cities on the map that are at sea level.

    _____

    _____

    b. Locate and circle Japan and Hawaii.

2. The colors on the color-code strip show the depths of the ocean.

    a. Circle the color on the strip that represents 20,000 feet or more.

    b. Draw an arrow from the strip you circled to cities on the map that are near that color.

3. Based on the fact that tsunamis originate in the deepest parts of the Pacific Ocean, in what places are earthquakes and volcanic eruptions likely to occur?

    _____

B. More than three fourths of the world's earthquakes occur around the Pacific Ocean. This area around the Pacific Ocean is called the "Ring of Fire" because of its frequent volcanic eruptions.

1. Describe how tsunamis, earthquakes, and volcanic eruptions are connected.

    _____

    _____

    _____

2. Explain why Japan, Alaska, and Hawaii's relative location makes them likely targets for tsunamis.

    _____

    _____

    _____

    _____

MAP SKILLS Using Special-Purpose Maps

The two maps shown below are **special-purpose maps,** which focus on a specific topic. One map shows the moisture, ice extent, and forests of North America during the Ice Age. The other map shows the same features for the present day. By looking at the shading on each map, you can see how different North America was during the Ice Age.

Map 1:
Ice Age Moisture and Vegetation

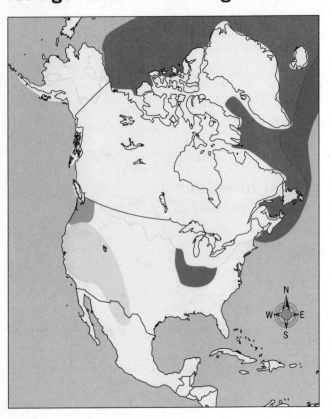

Map 2:
Present-Day Moisture and Vegetation

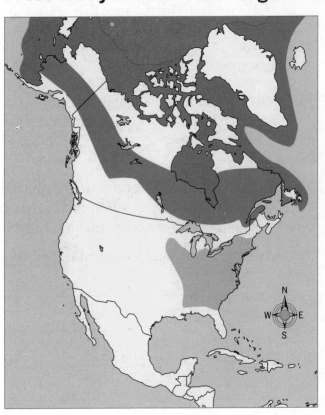

Map Key

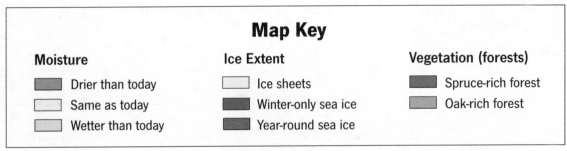

Moisture	Ice Extent	Vegetation (forests)
Drier than today	Ice sheets	Spruce-rich forest
Same as today	Winter-only sea ice	Oak-rich forest
Wetter than today	Year-round sea ice	

A. Study the climate and vegetation map of the Ice Age and answer the following questions.

1. What was the general moisture of North America like during the Ice Age?

   _____

2. What was the general moisture of present-day United States like during the Ice Age?

   _____

3. What was the primary vegetation during the Ice Age?

   _____

4. What part of present-day North America was covered with ice sheets?

   _____

B. Study the present-day climate and vegetation map to answer the following questions.

1. What is the primary vegetation in the United States on the present-day map?

   _____

2. Where is the spruce-rich forest today?

   _____

C. Use both climate and vegetation maps to answer the following questions.

1. How did the ice affect present-day vegetation?

   _____

   _____

2. How would you describe the change in the patterns of forests between the Ice Age period and present-day? Explain the role melted glacial ice played in the change in vegetation.

   _____

   _____

   _____

   _____

B. Think about where you live in the United States.

1. Write the names of the states near your state that you think have similar features—such as beaches, mountains, forests, or weather—to your state.

_____   _____

_____   _____

2. If you could give your state, together with the ones you listed above, a "region" name, what would you call the region? Think about features the states share and write a region name below.

_____

C. Looking at the map, think about what you know about the different areas of our country. What makes each area special or unique? How would you divide the United States into regions?

1. Write the names of the regions you would include. (Possible answers include the following.)

a. Southwest   d. Northeast

b. Midwest   e. Mid-Atlantic

c. Northwest   f. Southeast

2. Make notes about where you will draw the borders for each region.

(Students' answers might reflect boundaries that indicate a similarity in the land, water, resources, climate, and/or vegetation of states in an area.)

_____

_____

D. Compare your map with the regional maps in the article.

1. Does your map have the same number of regions?

2. Which, if any, borders are alike, and which are different? Why do you think the same or different borders were chosen?

(Students' answers should describe differences in borders of specific regions.)

_____

page 67

A. Study the physical map of California. Use the information on the map to complete the following.

1. Trace the line of the San Andreas Fault on the map.

2. How long is the San Andreas Fault? more than 750 miles long

3. What major cities are located on or near the fault? San Francisco, Oakland, Fremont, San Jose, San Bernardino, and Los Angeles

4. Write a brief desciption of where the fault is located, including where it begins and ends. The San Andreas Fault is located mainly on the western side of California. It reaches from near the Mexican border, up through San Francisco and Oakland, and into the Pacific Ocean.

B. Continue to study the map, particularly the San Andreas Fault. Complete the following.

1. Which California city has been hit by two severe earthquakes, one in 1906 and another in 1989? San Francisco

2. Use the chart below to describe the city, including where in California it is located and its land and water features.

City Name	San Francisco
Where It Is Located	toward northern California; between the Pacific Ocean and the San Francisco Bay; on the San Andreas Fault
Land and Water Features	hilly; almost completely surrounded by water

3. Do you think the city's location makes it more vulnerable to the activity of the San Andreas Fault than other cities located along the Fault? Why?
Yes, because it is the city most surrounded by water.

4. How does the San Andreas Fault affect life in California? It makes living in California dangerous because of the possibility of earthquakes and the destruction they cause.

page 69

A. Using the diagram, list the different forms of land and water in the appropriate columns below.

Landforms	Water Forms
butte	lagoon
cape	mouth
cliff	reservoir
delta	sound
dune	strait
mesa	tributary
reef	waterfall

B. Identify the landforms and water forms described below and complete the puzzle.

1. A stream that flows over the edge of a cliff. w a t e r f a l l

2. A narrow body of water that connects two larger bodies of water. s t r a i t

3. A river or stream that flows into a larger river or stream. t r i b u t a r y

4. The place where a river empties into a larger body of water. m o u t h

5. A point of land that extends into the water. c a p e

C. The following landforms and water forms are also on the map, but are not labeled. Label them. (Make sure students correctly identify the features listed below.)

1. mountain   6. volcano
2. river   7. glacier
3. ocean   8. bay
4. plateau   9. canal
5. hill   10. valley

D. Turn to the world map in the Almanac. How many other forms of land and water can you find? (Students might identify lake, gulf, island, peninsula, and so on.)

page 71

B. The map shows the routes of four famous expeditioners who went West. Using the map, answer the following questions.

1. Which explorer circled the land around the Great Basin?
Frémont

2. Which explorer traveled up the Arkansas River into the mountains, and then crossed the Rio Grande twice?
Pike

3. Choose one of the explorers listed on the map key. Write a description of the route he followed. What kinds of landforms did the explorer encounter?
(Students' descriptions should include information about physical features true to the chosen explorer's route.)

C. Physical features can be used as boundaries when dividing land. Suppose you were a settler traveling westward in the mid-1800s.

1. Choose a destination for your trip.
(Make sure students choose a territory west of the Mississippi River.)

2. What route would you follow to arrive at your destination?
(Make sure students' answers include a description of a route to get to their destination.)

3. What kind of land features might you find along the way?
(Such features should include the rivers; mountains; desert valleys; and dry, rugged plains that are indicated on the map.)

4. How might you use the land where you settle?
(Possible answers include: for farming, mining, trapping, raising cattle)

5. Your wagon train has a total of 30 wagons, each containing one family. Devise a method for dividing the land where you will settle. What boundaries will surround each family's plot of land? How will you decide what boundaries to use?
(Possible answers include: Boundaries may be determined by natural land features such as rivers, mountains or lakes; land may be divided along natural boundaries or along lines determined by law or agreement; land may be parceled out in square or rectangular lots.)

page 73

page 75

A. Look at the map of Europe. Circle the following cities and study their locations.
1. Zurich, Switzerland
2. Munich, Germany
3. Oslo, Norway
4. Copenhagen, Denmark
5. Dresden, Germany

B. Answer the following questions about the cities listed above.

1. Which of the five cities are landlocked? Dresden. Munich, and Zurich

2. What large bodies of water are the remaining two cities located near? Oslo is near the North Sea, while Copenhagen is on the Baltic Sea.

3. Between the two cities located near large bodies of water, which would you consider to be the most favorably located? Oslo

4. Why is the location of this city a favorable location? Oslo is located on an arm of the North Sea which flows into the Atlantic Ocean. Its location makes it easier for people and goods from different countries to get in and out of the city.

C. Analyze and indicate each city's location on the chart below. Then indicate on the chart the advantages and disadvantages of cities being located close to or far from these features.

Cities	Location	Advantages	Disadvantages
Zurich, Switzerland	central Europe near the Rhine River; in the Alps	mountains offer protection from invasion; center of Europe, crossroads of trade	difficult to travel through mountains; landlocked
Munich, Germany	southeastern Germany near the Danube River; in the foothills of the Alps	Danube River provides transportation link for trade and travel	foothills don't provide complete protection from invasion; landlocked
Oslo, Norway	southeastern Norway along the coast of the North Sea; no mountains	access to sea routes to Europe and the world through the North Sea	more open to invasion since it's accessible by sea and ocean
Copenhagen, Denmark	eastern coast of Denmark, at the entrance of the Baltic Sea; no mountains	controls entrance into Baltic Sea; ideal defensive position	being surrounded by water makes it hard for a city to expand; little unused land
Dresden, Germany	eastern Germany on the Elbe River; no mountains	the Elbe provides transportation links for trade and travel	difficult to defend because of its position with no natural barriers around it

page 75

page 77

A. Look at the map and answer the questions below.

1. List the nine islands that make up the state of Hawaii.
   a. Hawaii
   b. Kahoolawe
   c. Kauai
   d. Kaula
   e. Lanai
   f. Maui
   g. Molokai
   h. Nihau
   i. Oahu

2. Which color on the map represents the highest density, or concentration of people?
   purple

3. Which color represents the sparsely populated areas—areas with the fewest people?
   yellow

B. Urban means "in, of, or like a city." Rural means "in, of, or like the country." Use the map to answer the following questions.

1. Which map color would you say best represents urban areas? purple

2. Which color would you say best represents rural areas? yellow

3. How many people per square mile live on the northern tip of the island of Hawaii? 10 to 50 people per square mile

4. How do the coasts of the islands compare to the inland areas in population? In general, more people live on the coasts.

5. Which Hawaiian island has the highest population? Oahu

6. On which island are most of the cities located? Oahu

7. Compare the city locations with the population density and note your observations. Most cities are located along the coasts of the islands. These cities have the highest population densities.

page 77

page 79

A. Turn to the map of North America on page 4 in the Almanac. Notice the physical features of the following regions of the United States:
   Northwest—the Pacific Ocean and many rivers filled with fish, mountains thick with forests that provided timber for shelter and animals for food.
   Southwest—mostly desert with deep canyons and mountains; sun-baked soil provided raw material for shelters.
   Eastern Woodlands—dense with trees, rivers, swamps, and animal life.
   Great Plains—tall, vast grasslands provided home for roaming buffalo, which were a source of food, clothing, and shelter.
Circle and label these four regions on the map on page 78.

B. Compare the color patterns for high and low population densities on the map.

1. Which color represents a low population density? light yellow and gold

2. Which color represents a high population density? brown

3. Which areas of the United States had a low population density? Great Plains, Midwest, and parts of the Southwest

4. Which areas of the United States had a high population density? California and parts of the Northwest

C. Explain why some areas in the United States might have had an especially high population density. Base your answer on what you know about the geography and natural resources of the four regions prior to the time of Columbus.

(Students' answers should express the following idea: Areas with a lot of different food sources, such as fish and game, and plenty of materials for building might explain large communities being located there; whereas areas with only one or two food sources, such as the bison or a few plants and animals, and inadequate materials for building wouldn't support many communities. Also areas located near large bodies of water might have higher populations because the water could be used for drinking and transportation.)

page 79

page 81

A. Use the map to answer the following questions about specific location.

1. What city lies at a latitude of 41°N and a longitude of 74°W?
   New York City

2. About how many degrees of latitude are there between Philadelphia and New York City? one

3. About how many degrees of longitude are there between White Plains, New York and York, Pennsylvania? about 4 degrees

4. The Schuylkill River lies between what lines of latitude? 40N–41N

B. Look at the entire area that the map shows and answer the following questions.

1. About how many degrees of longitude does the map cover? 13

2. About how many degrees of latitude does the map cover? 10

C. Using the map, identify the places described below and answer the following questions.

1. If point A is located at 42°N and 75°W and point B is located at 40°N and 74°W, in what direction would you travel to get from point A to point B?
   southeast

2. Is there a city at 39°N and 74°W? If so, what city is it?
   No, that location is in the Atlantic Ocean.

3. About how many degrees of latitude are there between Yorktown, Virginia, and Philadelphia, Pennsylvania?
   about 3 degrees

4. What are the latitude and longitude coordinates for Lexington, Massachusetts?
   42°N and 71°W

5. What are the latitude and longitude coordinates for York, Pennsylvania?
   40°N and 78°W

page 81

A. Look at the map of Columbus' travels in 1492 and answer the following questions.

1. Columbus left Palos, Spain, on August 3, 1492. What is the approximate latitude of Palos, Spain?

   39°N

2. What is the approximate longitude of Palos, Spain? 7°W

3. What are the approximate latitude and longitude of the Canary Islands, where Columbus stopped in August 1492?

   29°N   16°W

4. If Columbus was at 30°N latitude and 60°W longitude, where would he be?

   in the Atlantic Ocean

5. At about what latitude was Columbus when he landed on San Salvador?

   24°N

6. Just south of San Salvador is a line of latitude with a special name. It is the northern boundary of the tropical region. What is this line of latitude called?

   Tropic of Cancer

7. If Columbus had landed at 30°N latitude on the North American continent, where would he have landed?

   present-day Florida

B. Looking at the map, number the following events of Columbus' journey in the correct order. Beside each different place where Columbus stopped, write its latitude and longitude.

Sequence	Events	Latitude and Longitude
3	Columbus lands at San Salvador Island.	24°N, 74°W
4	The Santa Maria goes aground on a reef.	
6	Two ships return to Palos.	37°N, 7°W
5	The Niña and Pinta begin their return voyage.	
2	Columbus reaches the Canary Islands.	29°N, 16°W
1	Columbus sails three ships out of port Palos, Spain.	37°N, 7°W

page 83

A. Use the time zone map to answer the following questions.

1. How many time zones are there in Australia?

   three

2. If it is 10 P.M. in Sydney, what time is it in Perth?

   8 P.M.

3. How many time zones are there in New Zealand?

   one

4. If it is 10 P.M. in Sydney, what time is it in Wellington, New Zealand?

   12 P.M.

The **international date line** is an imaginary line at 180° longitude that runs through the middle of the Pacific Ocean. By international agreement, it marks the spot where each new calendar day begins. Any time you cross the date line going from west to east, you move into the previous day (subtract one day). Anytime you cross the international date line going from east to west, you move into the following day (add one day). The time of day does not change. If you reach the date line at 4 P.M. on Tuesday coming from the east, it will be 4 P.M. Wednesday after you cross the line. If you cross back two hours later, it will be 6 P.M. on Tuesday.

B. With the previous information and the following scenario in mind, answer the questions below.

You are traveling from Western Samoa to Wellington, New Zealand. The trip takes four hours. You begin your trip at 7 A.M. on Saturday.

1. In which direction will you be traveling?

   southwest

2. How many time zones will you cross during your trip?

   one

3. Is New Zealand east or west of the international date line?

   west

4. What day and time will you arrive in Wellington, New Zealand?

   11 A.M. on Sunday

page 85

A. Look at the map of North America and answer the following questions.

1. What are the three countries of North America?

   Canada

   United States

   Mexico

2. What name is used to refer to the five lakes that form a boundary between Canada and the United States? Great Lakes

   Is it a natural or artificial boundary? natural

3. Name the river that forms a boundary between Mexico and the United States. Rio Grande

   Is it a natural or artificial boundary? natural

4. Name the area of land that is on the northwestern boundary of Canada and the country that owns that land. Alaska: the United States

   Is this a natural or artificial boundary? artificial

5. What is the number of the parallel line that forms a long section of the boundary between Canada and the United States? the 48th parallel

   Is this a natural or artificial boundary? artificial

B. Look at the coastline boundaries of North America and complete the following questions.

1. What ocean borders the east side of the United States and Canada? Atlantic Ocean

2. What ocean borders the west side of North America? Pacific Ocean

3. What ocean is north of Canada? Arctic Ocean

4. What large body of water lies between Mexico and the Atlantic Ocean? Gulf of Mexico

C. Draw some conclusions about the above information.

1. What does the map of North America tell you about boundaries? (Possible answer: Most of them seem to be natural boundaries like rivers and lakes; however, there are some artificial boundaries, too.)

2. Why do you think waterways are common boundaries in North America? People have historically settled near rivers, lakes, and streams that could be used for drinking water or transportation.

page 87

A. Look at the map and identify the following features.

1. Find an international boundary line and trace it with a red line.

2. Find the highway line and trace it with a yellow line.

3. Find the railroad line and trace it with a blue line.

4. Find the Trans-Alaska Pipeline and trace it with a green line.

B. Look at the legend on the map. Find these symbols and write what each one stands for.

1. ▪▪▪▪▪▪   railroad

2. ——   pipeline

3. ----   Dalton Highway

4. —   river

C. Use the map to answer these questions about international boundaries.

1. What country borders the east side of Alaska? Canada

2. How can you tell the boundary line between Alaska and that country?

   A line separating the two places is drawn on the map, and they are different colors.

3. What country borders the west side of Alaska? Russia

4. What body of water forms a boundary between Alaska and that country?

   the Bering Strait

D. Think about the boundaries between Alaska and Canada and Alaska and Russia. Write a few sentences explaining which is a physical boundary and which is a human boundary. Explain your answer.

The boundary between Alaska and Canada is a human-made boundary because it is a line that only shows up on a map drawn by people. The boundary between Alaska and Russia is a physical boundary because it is a body of water formed by nature.

page 89

page 91

A. List the six states shown on the map that make up the New England region. Then label them on the map.

1. Connecticut
2. New Hampshire
3. Maine
4. Massachusetts
5. Rhode Island
6. Vermont

B. Use information from the Internet or your local library and the Almanac to identify the following. After you identify these places, locate and label them on the map.

1. A name for the region of forests before European exploration
   Eastern Woodlands (New England)
   Trace this region on the map.

2. The mountains of eastern North America that run through
   New England   Appalachian Mountains
   Draw these mountains on the map.

3. The ocean that the explorers crossed to get to North America   Atlantic Ocean
   Label this ocean on the map.

4. The country that sent Giovanni da Verrazano and Samuel de Champlain
   to explore coastal New England   France
   Draw a line from this country to the New England region on the globe.

5. The country that sent John Smith to explore coastal New England   England
   Draw a line from this country to the New England region on the globe.

6. The harbor that Champlain mapped and described   Plymouth Harbor
   Label this harbor on the map.

7. The harbor that John Smith mapped and described   Boston Harbor
   Label this harbor on the map.

page 93

A. Look at the maps of southern Florida. Put an X on the following places on each map.

Map A
1. Lake Okeechobee
2. Big Cypress Swamp
3. Everglades
4. Kissimmee River

Map B
5. Florida Panther National Wildlife Refuge
6. Everglades National Park
7. Big Cypress National Preserve
8. Florida Trail

B. Use both maps to complete the following.

1. Indicate on which map you can find each of the following and whether each is natural or human-made.

   a. Big Cypress Swamp?   Map A; natural
   b. Orlando?   Map B; human-made
   c. Big Cypress National Preserve?   Map B; human-made
   d. an interstate highway?   Map B; human-made
   e. a canal?   Map B; human-made
   f. rivers?   Map A; natural

2. Look at Map B. Where are most of the cities located?
   Most cities are located along the coast and along the edges of the Big Cypress Swamp and the Everglades.

3. Draw the information from Map B onto Map A.
   a. Place the cities, roads, and canals on Map A.
   b. Add the boundaries to show Big Cypress National Preserve and Everglades National Park.
   c. Are any human-made features such as cities located inside Big Cypress National Preserve and Everglades National Park?   No

4. Now look at Map A. Describe how much of the Everglades and Big Cypress Swamp has been preserved by humans and what has happened to the remainder of the wetlands.
   (Students' descriptions should indicate that approximately one third of each wetlands environment has been preserved and the remainder has been drained for farming and development.)

page 95

A. On the map locate the waterways listed below. Draw a symbol to represent a strait next to each one.
1. Bosporus Strait
2. Dardanelles Strait
3. Strait of Gibraltar
4. Strait of Hormuz
5. Suez Canal

B. Use the map and Almanac information on pages 2, 3 and 4 to answer the following questions.

1. Would shipping be easier to block in the Gibraltar or Bosporus strait? Why?
   The Bosporus Strait would be easier to block because it is more narrow. It is only one half mile wide.

2. What countries rely on the Strait of Hormuz to ship their oil?   Iran, Iraq, Kuwait, Saudi Arabia, Qatar, the United Arab Emirates, and Bahrain

3. Why would Russia want control of the Bosporus Strait?   The Bosporus Strait gives Russia access to the Mediterranean Sea, and from there to the Atlantic Ocean and the Suez Canal. This would make it easier for Russia to ship goods to other countries of the world.

4. How is the Suez Canal different from the straits in this area of the world?   It was not a natural strait but a waterway built by man. It serves the same function as a strait.

5. Why is the Suez Canal important to Israel?   It gives Israel easier and quicker access to the Red Sea, Indian Ocean, and countries in eastern Asia.

6. How was the Strait of Hormuz important to the countries involved in the Persian Gulf War?   The Strait of Hormuz allowed United States military troops to enter the Persian Gulf, and eventually Saudi Arabia, during the Gulf War. Coming into Saudi Arabia from the coast of the Persian Gulf was easier for the troops because they didn't have to travel through the desert in southern Saudi Arabia.

7. Why has the Dardanelles Strait been important throughout history?   The Dardanelles Strait has been important for defense and military campaigns because it provides a short passage between Europe and southwest Asia.

page 97

A. List the major cities along the fall line.

Macon, GA
Columbia, SC
Baltimore, MD
Philadelphia, PA
Raleigh, NC
Richmond, VA
New York City, NY

B. Look at the map and write down the approximate elevations of the following cities.

1. Raleigh, North Carolina   0–500 feet
2. Pittsburgh, Pennsylvania   1,000–2000 feet
3. Baltimore, Maryland   0–500 feet
4. Columbia, South Carolina   0–500 feet

C. Look at the fall line on the map. Answer the following questions.

1. Explain why Raleigh, Baltimore, and Columbia are fall line cities.
   Due to their low elevation and position on the Atlantic Coastal plain, these cities developed along the fall line.

2. Explain why Pittsburgh is not a fall line city.
   Pittsburgh is located in a hills region of western Pennsylvania on the western side of the Appalachian Mountains. It has a high elevation. Fall line cities have lower elevations. They are located on the Atlantic Coastal Plains.

D. In the twentieth century, industry has developed in all regions of the United States. Explain why industry is no longer dependent on physical features such as the eastern fall line.
   Technology has advanced. We no longer have to depend solely on waterpower as an energy source.

125

A. Look at the elevation key to answer the following questions.
1. Write the elevation of the land shown in yellow.

____152____ meters ____500____ feet

2. Which elevation is higher, the light green area or the orange area?

the orange area

B. Look at the map of the Middle Atlantic region.
1. What is the elevation of most of the land along the Atlantic Ocean?

0 meters, 0 feet, sea level

2. Describe how the land changes as you travel from west to east.

(Students should describe the gradual change from mountains of around 1,000 feet in

elevation to land at sea level at the Atlantic Ocean.)

C. Find Buffalo, New York, on Lake Erie. Draw a line from west to east going from Buffalo to Albany, New York.
1. What two colors do you pass through? What are the elevations?

a. Elevation color	**b.** Elevation in feet
orange	1,000 feet
yellow	500 feet

2. What is the name of the mountain range north of the line that you drew?

Adirondack Mountain Range

3. Continue your line from Albany, New York, by tracing the Hudson River south to New York City. What is the elevation in feet? 0 feet or sea level

4. Do you think the route from Buffalo to Albany was a good route for the Erie Canal? Why? (Students should mention that the route followed the least change in elevation,

which made it an easier route to build the Erie Canal.)

page 99

A. Study the elevation key on the map of Europe and Asia. Use the key and the map to help you identify the following features.
1. How did you use the map to help you identify:
   a. mountain ranges?

   looked for the color shadings that represented areas of high elevation

   b. plains?

   looked for the color shadings that represented areas of low elevation

2. Define and distinguish between a peninsula and an island.

Peninsulas are extensions connected to the land and are surrounded by water on three sides. Islands

are surrounded by water on all sides.

B. Look at the map and complete the following.
1. Draw a line showing where Europe and Asia are divided.
2. Using the map, write a description of the physical features you see in Europe.

Europe is the western portion of the Eurasia landmass. It has some high mountains and is

surrounded by water on three sides. It has many small peninsulas along its coastline and plains

on its interior.

3. Why do you think Europe is considered a peninsula of Asia, rather than Asia being considered a peninsula of Europe?

Asia is a larger piece of land, and Europe appears to jut out from Asia.

4. Write a description of the physical features of Asia.

Asia is a huge landmass with some high mountains, uplands, and highlands. However, large areas of

Asia's land are plains and plateaus. Its eastern coastline is bordered by many islands.

5. Describe the physical features that are shared by both Europe and Asia.

Europe and Asia share the Ural Mountains and a huge plains area. The North European Plain on

the Europe side of the Urals becomes the West Siberian Plain on the Asia side of the Urals. The two

continents also share the Caspian and Black seas as partial borders between them.

page 101

A. Look at the political and physical map of south Asia and complete the following.
1. List the six countries shown.

Bangladesh	Nepal
Bhutan	Pakistan
India	Sri Lanka

2. Name the three large bodies of water that border south Asia.

Indian Ocean, Arabian Sea, and the Bay of Bengal

3. What are the three major mountain ranges that surround India?

Western Ghats, Eastern Ghats, and the Himalayas

4. What are the three main rivers in south Asia?

Ganges, Indus, and the Brahmaputra

B. Look for the precipitation and vegetation maps of India in the Almanac. Precipitation maps show the amount of rainfall an area receives. Vegetation maps show how plant life responds to climatic conditions. Complete the following.
1. Which parts of India receive the most rainfall?

the western coast of India and parts of northeast

2. What type of vegetation is found in the areas with the most rainfall?

broadleaf evergreen, broadleaf deciduous, and mixed deciduous and evergreen trees

3. Describe the general relationship between high levels of rainfall and vegetation.

Large amounts of rain produce thick vegetation.

C. Make connections among what you have learned about rainfall, vegetation, and physical features. Answer the following questions.
1. What kinds of physical features are located on the western coast and north-eastern coasts of India?

mountains

2. How do these physical features affect rainfall during the monsoon season?

Mountain slopes lift warm, moist air from the ocean to higher altitudes. The air

cools and forms clouds that produce rain.

page 103

A. Look at the map and circle the following.

1. Illinois	3. Nebraska	5. Missouri
2. Iowa	4. Arizona	6. Map key

B. Use the map and map key to answer the following questions.
1. a. What does a red dot mean? _____10,000 acres of corn_____

   b. What does a green dot mean? _____20,000 acres of wheat_____

2. a. Name at least five states where corn is grown. Illinois, Iowa, Wisconsin, Ohio, Nebraska,

   Kansas, Missouri, Minnesota, and South Dakota

   b. How do you know corn is grown in the states you named? The red dots and Corn Belt

   label indicate where corn is grown.

C. Answer the following.
1. How many dots do you see in Arizona? 3
2. What color is each dot? There is a red dot, a light green dot, and a dark green dot.

3. How many acres of corn are grown in Arizona? 10,000 acres

   How do you know? The map key shows that one red dot is equal to 10,000 acres of corn.

4. Is more corn grown in Arizona or Illinois? Illinois

   Explain how you know. There are many more red dots in Illinois than in Arizona.

D. Write a few sentences comparing the amount of corn grown in Ohio to the amount of corn grown in Missouri.

Ohio and Missouri seem to grow almost the same amount of corn. Ohio's corn seems to

be grown all over the state, whereas Missouri's corn seems to be grown mostly in the

northern part of the state.

page 105

page 107

2. Name two farm products raised in the 1700s by settlers from each of the following countries. (Students' answers might include the following.)

   a. England   tobacco, cattle, corn, wheat, swine, sheep, rice

   b. France   cattle, corn, hemp, rice, swine

   c. Spain   cattle, sheep, corn

3. Some of the resources the settlers found did not have to be grown, but still came from the land. These types of resources are raw materials. Name two kinds of raw materials found in the 1700s by settlers from each of the following countries. (Students' answers might include the following.)

   a. England   wood products, iron

   b. France   iron, furs, indigo

   c. Spain   wood products, indigo, gold and silver

4. List below each of the products you named above and how Europeans and Native Americans might have used these farm products.
   (Make sure students' descriptions of each product's use correspond with the product.)

Farm Products	European Uses	Native American Uses

5. Which group of early colonists relied most heavily on farming?   the English

6. Which group of early settlers relied most heavily on the land's raw materials?   the French

7. Do you think the Spanish, French, and English settlers used more of the products they raised in North America or traded more with their native countries? Explain your answer.

   (Students' answers should indicate that the Europeans traded more of their products with their native countries for profit than they did with each other in North America.)

page 109

A. Look at the map and complete the following.
   1. Underline the names of the states in the northern spring wheat belt.
   2. Circle the names of the states in the southern winter wheat belt.

B. Answer the following questions about where the different kinds of wheat are grown.

   1. Which two states grow the most wheat? Kansas and North Dakota

   2. Which states produce both spring and winter wheat? Washington, Oregon, Idaho, Montana, and South Dakota

   3. Which states are minor producers of winter wheat? Wisconsin, Iowa, Indiana, Michigan, Ohio, Tennessee, North Carolina, South Carolina, Georgia, New York, Pennsylvania, Virginia, Kentucky, California, Arizona, Utah, New Mexico

   4. Is there more winter wheat or spring wheat grown in the United States? winter wheat

   5. Which three spring wheat producing states grow the smallest amount of spring wheat?
   Washington, Oregon, and Idaho

   6. Where in North America is the most spring wheat grown?
   northern United States and southern Canada

page 111

A. Using the map legend, make a list of the resources found in the area of Kenya near Lake Victoria. Remember that resources can include crops, animals, minerals, and natural features that might promote tourism.

cattle	diamonds
coffee	Lake Victoria
copper	national parks
cotton	sugarcane

B. Think about the resources found in the Lake Victoria area and answer the following questions.
   1. The land used for farming around Lake Victoria is very dry. When there is no rain, crops such as corn will not grow, and the people have no food. What available resource could farmers use to water their corn in times of low rainfall? How would they transport the resource?

   People could build irrigation systems using the water from the lake.

   2. Nile perch were added to Lake Victoria so the area would have a product that could be exported. Describe alternative ways that people might have improved the economy of the area.

   (Possible answers include: With irrigation the people could have increased the yield of crops that already grew well, such as tea, coffee, and sugarcane; Lake Victoria could have been developed into a tourist attraction with beaches, fishing trips, resorts, treks to see exotic animals, or hikes to nearby mountains and national parks.)

   3. List advantages and disadvantages for each of your answers to question 2.

   (Possible answers include the following.

   Irrigating the land: Advantage—This would provide plenty of water to grow lots of native crops.

   Disadvantage—It would cost a lot of money to build the system.

   Make Lake Victoria a tourist attraction: Advantage—This would bring people and money into an area and provide an opportunity to share information about the importance of preserving the area.

   Disadvantage—It would cost a lot to build hotels and fix up beaches, and it might change the character of the area.)

page 113

A. Use the map scale to answer the following questions.
   1. How many miles are represented on the scale?
   200

   2. Using a ruler and the map scale to determine the distance, approximately how many miles by air is Boston from New York City?
   approximately 200 miles

B. Use a piece of string and a ruler to measure the distance by water between Boston and Cape Hatteras on the map and answer the following questions.

   1. How many inches is the length of string that represents the distance from Boston to Cape Hatteras? 3 inch(es)

   2. Measure the miles line on the map scale. Complete the following.
   1 inch(es) is equal to 200 miles.

   3. How many miles by water is Boston from Cape Hatteras? approximately 600 miles

C. Use a string and the map scale to measure and determine the distance of the land and water routes between Boston and Houston.

   1. How long is the land route from Boston to Houston? approximately 1,875 miles

   2. How long is the water route from Boston to Houston? approximately 2,500 miles

   3. If you had been traveling in the 1400s from what is now Boston to what is now Houston, which route would you have taken? Think about the ways people traveled during that time. Explain your answer.
   (Students' answers should reflect their understanding that the water route would have been faster because efficient ships were available. There were no roads.)

   4. If you were traveling from Boston to Houston in the 1990s, would you take the water or land route? Explain why.
   (Students' answers might be that they would take the land route because there are good roads and good automobiles. The water route would be possible, but there is little passenger travel along this route. It would be expensive and time consuming.)

A. Study the map. Using different colored pencils for each item listed below, circle the following on the map. (Make sure students locate and circle the following items on the map.)
1. Windhoek, Namibia and Gabarone, Botswana
2. Kalahari Desert
3. Towns or settlements along the northern route between Windhoek and Gabarone

B. Use the map, scale, and legend to complete the following.
1. If you were flying from Windhoek directly to Gabarone, how many miles would you travel?

   about 550 miles

2. What other two methods of transportation could be used to get from Windhoek to Gabarone? In different colors, trace these two routes on your map.

   railroad and roads

3. What form of transportation and route would be the quickest and easiest to travel from Windhoek to Gabarone, and how many miles would the route be?

   The road route by car from Windhoek, through the towns of Gobabis, Maun, Francistown, and

   Mahalapye would be the quickest and easiest. This route would be about 1,080 miles.

4. Describe the physical features you would encounter as you travel from east to west.

   a desert, lake, and swamp

5. What supplies would you need to take with you on your trip using the quickest and easiest route? Explain your answer.

   (Students should indicate that they need to take extra water and food, light-weight clothes, and

   protection from the sun because they have to travel through the Kalahari Desert.)

6. What form of transportation and route would be the longest and hardest to travel from Windhoek to Gabarone, and how many miles would the route be?

   The train route southward through the mountains would be the longest and hardest. This route would

   be about 1,180 miles. The train would probably travel slower than a car, and traveling through the

   mountains would make it even slower. Plus, there are no places to stop along the way.

page 115

A. Study the map and the precipitation key.
1. What areas have the highest average precipitation? the areas along the Pacific Coast

2. What physical features are found in or near the areas that have the highest

   precipitation? mountains and rivers

3. What areas show the lowest average precipitation? the central and eastern parts of Oregon

4. What physical features are found in the areas that have the lowest

   precipitation? mountains, rivers, a desert, and a basin

B. The occurrence of heavy rainfall in western Oregon and dry climate in eastern Oregon is due to *orographic precipitation*, which occurs when warm air is forced upward by a rise in land, such as a hill or mountain. As the warm air rises and meets the cool air over the mountain, precipitation is released and the air becomes dry before traveling down the other side. Draw a diagram of this process in the appropriate place on the map on page 116.
1. What happens to the air as it moves up the ocean side of the mountain?

   The air gets cooler as it flows up the mountain.

2. Where does it rain? It rains on the ocean side of the mountain.

3. What is the air like as it moves down the far side of the mountain?

   The air is drier. It gets warmer as it flows down the mountain.

page 117

A. Maps show ocean depth and area at sea level. Study the map and legend and complete the following.
1. The cities on the map are at sea level, the place where land is the same height as the sea.

   a. List the cities on the map that are at sea level.

   Tokyo, Honolulu, San Francisco, San Diego, Los Angeles, Aleutian Islands, and Seattle

   b. Locate and circle Japan and Hawaii. (Make sure students accurately circle these islands.)

2. The colors on the color-code strip show the depths of the ocean. (Make sure students accurately complete the following.)

   a. Circle the color on the strip that represents 20,000 feet or more.

   b. Draw an arrow from the strip you circled to cities on the map that are near that color.

3. Based on the fact that tsunamis originate in the deepest parts of the Pacific Ocean, in what places are earthquakes and volcanic eruptions likely to occur?

   Tokyo, Japan; Aleutian Islands, Alaska; and Honolulu, Hawaii

B. More than three fourths of the world's earthquakes occur around the Pacific Ocean. This area around the Pacific Ocean is called the "Ring of Fire" because of its frequent volcanic eruptions.
1. Describe how tsunamis, earthquakes, and volcanic eruptions are connected.

   Tsunamis, earthquakes, and volcanic eruptions are all disruptive tremors or movements that occur on

   the surface of Earth. They all occur along the "Ring of Fire," along the Pacific Ocean and are very

   destructive.

2. Explain why Japan, Alaska, and Hawaii's relative location makes them likely targets for tsunamis.

   Japan and Alaska are located near the deepest parts of the Pacific Ocean, within an earthquake zone

   and near active volcanoes which create tsunamis. Hawaii is surrounded by these faraway tsunami,

   causing earthquake zones and volcanoes.

page 119

A. Study the climate and vegetation map of the Ice Age and answer the following questions.
1. What was the general moisture of North America like during the Ice Age?

   same as today

2. What was the general moisture of present-day United States like during the Ice Age?

   wetter than today

3. What was the primary vegetation during the Ice Age?

   spruce-rich forest

4. What part of present-day North America was covered with ice sheets?

   northeastern United States and Canada

B. Study the present-day climate and vegetation map to answer the following questions.
1. What is the primary vegetation in the United States on the present-day map?

   oak-rich forest

2. Where is the spruce-rich forest today?

   Canada and Alaska

C. Use both climate and vegetation maps to answer the following questions.
1. How did the ice affect present-day vegetation?

   The ice melted, producing water that created spruce-rich forest in Canada and oak-rich

   forest in the eastern United States.

2. How would you describe the change in the patterns of forests between the Ice Age period and present-day? Explain the role melted glacial ice played in the change in vegetation.

   During the Ice Age, the ice sheet extended as far south as the Midwest, covering the Great

   Lakes, with a few spruce-rich forests below that point. In the present day, much of the ice

   sheet has melted, uncovering the midwestern United States and Canada, causing spruce-rich

   forests to grow across Canada and oak-rich forests to grow in the eastern United States.

page 121

128